Phantom Calls

Los Angeles Lakers' Shaquille O'Neal (34) defends as Houston Rockets' Yao Ming (11), of China, shoots during the first quarter in Game 3 of the first-round Western Conference NBA playoffs Friday, April 23, 2004, in Houston. Copyright ©2004 AP Photo/David J. Phillip, used by permission.

Phantom Calls:
Race and the Globalization of the NBA

Grant Farred

PRICKLY PARADIGM PRESS
CHICAGO

Prickly Paradigm Press, LLC
5629 South University Avenue
Chicago, Il 60637

www.prickly-paradigm.com

ISBN: 0-9761475-3-X
LCCN: 2006903876

Printed in the United States of America on acid-free
paper.

For Walt "Clyde" Frazier,
the greatest New York Knick of all,
whose radio commentaries provide
a basketball education

Introduction

A phantom speaks. What does this mean?
                                        Jacques Derrida,
                    Archive Fever: A Freudian Impression

In Game Five of the 2004-05 National Basketball
Association playoffs, the Houston Rockets' star
Chinese center, Yao Ming, was called for a series of
fouls against the Dallas Mavericks. Yao seemed
perplexed by the calls, a little upset, even, but his coach
Jeff Van Gundy was beside himself with anger. After
the game, which the Rockets lost despite a solid effort
from Yao, a livid Van Gundy accused the referees of
making "phantom calls" against Yao. Van Gundy's

statements set off a furor, not only within NBA circles but far beyond them. The controversy extended from Houston, Texas, to Shanghai, China—Yao's hometown—incorporating within its arc explosive issues of race, ethnicity, nationalism, and the workings of early twenty-first-century global capitalism.

In as much, however, as there is something strange about Yao's capacity to raise these issues, there is also, paradoxically, something historically appropriate about a Chinese player revealing the Phantoms that lurk in the American socio-political psyche. After all, basketball arrived in China decades before any Texan imagined a professional franchise in Houston: In fact, while the Chinese star Yao was drafted by the Houston Rockets in June 2002, the game had arrived in China not long after its invention in 1891. The NBA may well be a globalized league today, but basketball was a sport global in its reach almost from the moment of its late-nineteenth century inception.

Basketball was founded by Canadian-born James Naismith in New England in the winter of 1891. The sport was popular from the start, from the moment that Naismith hung two peach baskets at the end of a makeshift "court" at the Young Men's Christian Association (YMCA) in Springfield, Massachusetts. Naismith was not trying to create a new game—sports historian Peter Bjarkman calls it "America's most native game"—he was simply trying to provide indoor exercise for gridiron players when it was too cold to go outside. Little did Naismith know that within a few years, basketball would reach the Far East. Yao's arrival in the NBA, however, could be attributed less to Naismith than to the evangelical politics of the YMCA (leaving aside, momentarily, the NBA's decades-old desire to expand its market to China). It was Christian missionaries, trained in the skills of basketball in precisely the kind of gym where Naismith routinely held court, who exported the Canadian's game to China. Armed with no literature other than the Bible and a booklet entitled "The Thirteen Rules of Basketball," professing a muscular Christianity among a colonized people deeply insecure about their own physiological prowess, the YMCA missionaries tried to recruit souls while teaching the natives a game they themselves had as yet barely mastered.

If the late-nineteenth century missionary politics of the YMCA explains Yao's twenty-first century arrival in the NBA, his status as minority can only be explained by mapping briefly the racial and socio-economic history of US basketball in the twentieth century. Professional basketball in America was not always the lucrative, glamorous enterprise it is today; its roots are much more humble, demonstrating a history filled with struggles to survive economically. While Yao entered the globalized, supposedly post-racial NBA, still dominated by the aura of Michael Jordan, the previous century had been marked by the struggles of the league's dominant minority—African Americans. Black players had fought racial discrimination to secure their right to participate as equals in not only basketball, but all American sport. The road from Springfield to Shanghai, from the African-American Michael Jordan to the Asian Yao Ming, runs not only from the YMCA through state-run Chinese basketball to the NBA, but also through the historic event of Jackie Robinson and the integration of American baseball.

As basketball was establishing itself in Asia, the "game spread like wildfire" in the US, according to Bjarkman in *The History of the NBA*. Early in the twentieth century, basketball was adopted by American colleges while barnstorming leagues became a staple of the American entertainment industry. In fact, basketball games often took place in ballrooms, providing the warm-up acts for dancing or big band music. It was from one such venue, the Renaissance Casino Ballroom, that the all-black New York Renaissance (the "Rens") took their name. For decades after its creation, however, basketball remained a haphazard enterprise—franchises came and went, all too quickly, leagues starting and folding, sometimes equally quickly. During that period, basketball wended its way through the American heartland, reaching such small Midwestern towns as Sheboygan and Oshkosh.

It was only after World War II that professional basketball began to come into its own. And, even that early incarnation of the NBA—with its small audiences in small cities such as Syracuse and Fort Wayne, paltry salaries, and flat profits—is galaxies removed from what it would become in the 1980s and '90s. Energized by the "Magic" Johnson-Larry Bird rivalry, and then electrified by the unimagined brilliance of Michael Jordan, the NBA would have been largely unrecognizable to those athletes who competed in the league's formative years. After Magic and Bird entered the NBA in 1979, the league produced a style of basketball that enthralled fans (and players), literally, across the globe. It made NBA stars household names (with Jordan undeniably on top, although with room for others) from Chicago to Kingston to Kinshasa. (This list includes the tough, competitive star centers Moses Malone and Patrick Ewing who would later, in different capacities, work with Yao.)

This was a far cry from the NBA's founding in 1949, established out of the merger between the Basketball Association of America (BAA) and the National Basketball League (NBL). Its first Commissioner, Maurice Podoloff, was—fittingly—a Canadian. In addition to administering the new league, Podoloff's other great accomplishment was overseeing its racial integration. Although African Americans had been playing basketball since its inception, boasting well-known professional franchises such as the Rens and the Harlem Globetrotters (who were actually from Chicago), in its first year the NBA was segregated.

Because basketball is not "America's game" (that honor, alas, goes to baseball), its integration was neither as spectacular as Jackie Robinson's introduction into the Major Leagues nor as memorialized as the event of a lone black man taking the field for the Brooklyn Dodgers in that 1947 game against the Boston Braves. And yet, even that signal moment in American cultural life, as the San Francisco Giants' star outfielder Barry Bonds argued just a few years ago, is a socio-political landmark now lost to most players, fans, and administrators. Today, many players have no idea as to who Jackie Robinson is or what he meant to the game.

Even more disregarded and little known is the story of basketball's integration. It is a legacy that has disappeared into the mists of cultural time and is recalled now only by sports historians and old-time African-American players like Wayne Embry (the center for the Cincinnati Royals from the late-1950s through the mid-1960s). But on April 25, 1950, Boston drafted the NBA's first black player—Charles Cooper, out of Dusquesne University—early in the second round of the draft. In the ninth round, Washington selected Earl Lloyd out of West Virginia State; and, finally, New York bought out the contract of Nat "Sweetwater" Clifton from its neighbors, the Harlem Globetrotters. There is, in Embry's polemically sub-titled autobiography, *The Inside Game: Race, Power, and Politics in the NBA*, an unmistakable pride in the recollection of that historic moment.

It is for this reason that, despite the discrepancy between the cultural significance afforded them, these moments of sports integration are so inextricably linked. It was Jackie Robinson's breaking the color barrier that made Cooper's, Lloyd's and Clifton's careers in the NBA possible—and, Embry knew, his own. An old-school player, bruising and combative as the Royals' undersized (6'8") center, Embry represents a generation of professional African-American athletes (in both basketball and baseball) who understood, both because of their historical proximity to and their coming-of-age in the Civil Rights era, the magnitude of their colleagues' achievements. After Robinson took the field for the Brooklyn Dodgers, professional basketball had little choice but to follow suit. The integration of the NBA in 1950 meant, inevitably, the collapse of history-filled professional black franchises, as Washington, Boston, and New York began to raid them for their talent. Of those outfits, it is only the Globetrotters who have survived in any sustainable form, and then only as a minstrel sideshow to the NBA—an all-too-colorful incarnation of their once splendid, barnstorming, and highly competitive selves. Also disappearing quickly, though not as quickly as the integration narrative, are recollections of the NBA before its Magic-Bird-Jordan days. Consigned to the dustbin of basketball history are players and teams foundational to the current league. Players such as the original "big man," George Mikan. At 6'10", Mikan, a "Goliath in canvas sneakers," was professional basketball's first "big man," dominating both the NBL and the NBA, winning a handful of championships in each. A graduate of De Paul University, Mikan anchored the NBA's first dynasty, the Minneapolis Lakers, winning four championships in the period between 1950 and 1955.

Mikan's success with the Lakers was quickly eclipsed, however, by the rise of arguably the greatest dynasty in the NBA: the Boston Celtics. The utter domination of Bill Russell's Celtics from 1957 to 1969 was such that those years in basketball history earned a singular sobriquet: the "Celtic Mystique." Coached until 1966 by the cigar-puffing Red Auerbach, the Celtics swept all before them during that glorious era. Also of no small historical significance was the decision by Auerbach to appoint, in the summer of 1966, Bill Russell as player-coach, making Russell the first black coach in the history of the NBA. With the likes of Bob Cousy, John Havlicek, Tom Heinsohn, and Sam Jones starring, the Celtics were the envy of all other teams. The most memorable aspect of that era, of course, is the rivalry between Russell and Wilt Chamberlain, the latter a flamboyant center for Philadelphia and then the Los Angeles Lakers. But Wilt—such an offensive force that he once scored 100 points in a single game—lost every time to Russell's Celtics.

Were it not for how ESPN's *Sportscenter* has valorized the dunk, Julius Erving's days as the star attraction in the American Basketball Association in the early 1970s would long since have been allowed to fade entirely from public memory. Under similar threat are Lew Alcindor's (later Kareem Abdul-Jabbar) brilliant college career and the elegance—capped by his signature "baby sky hook," a shot deemed "indefensible" by his opponents—he brought to the center position in his time with the Bucks and the Lakers. Those days are now the stuff of the ESPN archives and nostalgia.

And, finally, the scandal of rampant drug use in the NBA from the mid-1970s to the early 1980s is now nothing but a faintly odorous whiff, cleansed by the tough administration of Commissioner David Stern. The drug allegations were not uninformed by how "black" the league had become in the decades since its founding. A lawyer, Stern is credited with saving the NBA from disrepute, ignominy, lost TV revenues, and a propensity for self-destruction. So precipitously had the status of the NBA declined that the 1980 finals between Los Angeles and Philadelphia was only shown on tape delay, after midnight, on CBS. Stern is, of course, fortunate to have taken up the Commissioner's job at the right time. He became Commissioner in 1983, the year before Jordan entered the NBA and just as the league was recovering from the "lost decade" of the 1970s. The NBA was on the road to improved health courtesy of the bi-coastal, barely disguised racial rivalry between Magic and Bird.

This contest pitted the putatively "white" Celtics (actually filled with black players and headed by a black coach) versus the "black" Lakers (coached by Pat Riley, a white graduate of the University of Kentucky, where Coach Adolph Rupp had believed firmly in the virtues of segregation). Flashy, highly stylized in their on- and off-court moves, and led by the ever-smiling Magic, with Abdul-Jabbar his stalwart center, the Lakers were the progenitors of NBA hype and cool. For all their importance in resurrecting the NBA's fortunes, however, Magic and Bird were doing little more than playing a bi-racial John the Baptist to the True (black) Savior.

The phenomenon that was, and in some ways still is, Michael Jordan, was of course absolutely central to the NBA's revitalization. Jordan alone was responsible for the league's growth and, from the late-1980s, its expansion into a global enterprise. If the Celtics-Lakers rivalry had provided the NBA with a new cultural and economic foundation, it was Jordan who opened it to a whole new cultural and economic stratosphere. His Airness gave the NBA access to the whole world. According to Walter LaFeber, it was "his success in the global market that set Jordan apart." Jordan made the NBA global; he played in the NBA but he belonged to the world. Jordan not only belonged to the moment of transformation from a national to a global league, he was its grandest fulfillment. His Airness made possible the infinite international growth of the NBA. His career was emblematic of the explosive growth of neo-liberal capitalism from the 1980s on.

This was the decade of Reagan. To borrow a phrase from Gordon Gecko, the character in *Wall Street*, it was the decade in which "greed" was "good," in which it was imagined that capital could proliferate endlessly. It was a "me-first," acquisitive ethos that Jordan and the NBA understood perfectly. It also took that mantra to heart as the league secured its standing as a prime-time cultural event and set its sights on expansion, both nationally and internationally. For Stern, the world was nothing but a market to be cornered, a series of places where the NBA could sell its products and itself as consumable merchandise. With Europe already providing a steady stream of players, Stern took aim at the rest of the world. Early in his tenure, the Commissioner expressed his interest in China, already in the mid-1980s promising to be the biggest market of all. Jordan joined the Chicago Bulls in 1984 as an almost-post-Cold-War world was beginning to take shape. This was a world in which the flows of global capital and its capacity to proliferate his image enabled Jordan to transcend his North Carolina roots and his Chicago Bulls affiliation. *He* was *Michael Jordan*; the Bulls, at best, his supporting cast, at worst, merely the platform for his greatness. Most saliently, the Sternian ethos allowed him to transcend American society itself. By the end of his career in 2003, Jordan was one of the most recognized American athletes in the world.

Jordan was the athlete who single-handedly changed—well, with the help of Nike, McDonalds, Wheaties, Hanes, and his innumerable other endorsements—the way capital and sport interact. Over the course of some two decades, Jordan was the pivotal figure in a triangulated commercial marriage, a ménage-a-trois composed of the NBA, the media, and his own iconic presence, that spawned millions of dollars for all concerned. Basketball quickly became one of the most lucrative sports in the world, making billions of dollars every year for franchises, players, coaches, media networks, advertisers, and sponsors from Beijing to Barcelona to Buenos Aires. Jordan's rise as a global icon has been like Manna from Heaven for the NBA.

Basketball has a long "international" history, but the post-Jordan NBA is the game's first real global force. By the 04-05 season, the NBA could boast that its teams featured 81 international players from 35 countries. Representatives from Argentina to Turkey, from Croatia to Slovenia, from the Congo to Spain, filled its ranks. The globalization of the NBA is most obviously demonstrated in the annual draft day proceedings. Whereas in 1994 only four foreign players were drafted, this number had increased to 10 just five years later.

In June 2005, 18 foreign-born players were selected, including Australia's Andrew Bogut, who was taken by the Milwaukee Bucks as the number one pick. The expansion of US culture and capital into every corner of the basketball-playing world has succeeded in globalizing the NBA. In return, of course, the world is increasingly being NBA'ed: from one continent to another, basketball products, sneakers, replica outfits, baseball hats, and all kinds of paraphernalia have become highly desired consumable objects; all, of course, with the attendant hip-hop culture in tow—the eye-catching tattoos, the hairstyles, the "street" language, and the flashy jewelry. Moreover, basketball is beginning to displace once-dominant traditional sports. In the Anglophone Caribbean, administrators worry for the future of cricket, as young Jamaicans and Trinidadians begin to have hoop dreams; in China, the days of football's (soccer's) hegemony are passing as the sport takes second place while basketball courts sprout up like mushrooms in Shanghai and Beijing.

What the NBA did not expect in the wake of its internationalization, however, were the ways in which the post-Jordan globalization era would unexpectedly resurrect one of the ghosts that His Airness' benign presence had supposedly laid to rest: the Phantom of race. The Phantom is that unspeakable aspect of the political that is feared because of its capacity to disrupt the "normal" functioning of a society; the Phantom is feared because its presence not only haunts the body politic, but is palpably present even when its disorderly propensities are not at work.

The Phantom, in literary terms, resembles the ghost of the dead king in *Hamlet*, and the historic aftereffects of slavery in Ralph Ellison's *Invisible Man*, and the murdered child in Toni Morrison's *Beloved*. They all give the living nary a moment's peace. In the post-Jordan NBA, race functions as a socio-political force. It compels, often in unexpected ways, a re-engagement with the effects of a segregated, discriminatory, and inequitable past. Rendered momentarily inactive by the Jordanesque discourse of post-racialism, it returns now to recall the ghosts of Clifton et al.

The Phantom is a threat because it resides in the self's relationship with the others who so closely resemble it—those to whom the self is bonded, like Russell to Wilt, Bird to Magic, Yao to his Chinese alter-ego, Wang. Antagonists, opponents, countrymen: the ghosts of others are lodged deep in the psyche of the self. It is for this reason that the Phantom is always only a crisis, an event, an evocation, removed from reactivation and rearticulation. Increasingly, as the NBA draft has become more international, so has the Phantom of race reemerged, reanimating that divisive aspect of the NBA's past that the Jordan era was supposed to have buried. "The foreign invasion," writes *Newsweek* journalist Brooks Larmer, "naturally, has its critics, from those who moan about the NBA's eagerness to exploit overseas markets to those who say it is part of a 'pearl drops' strategy to whiten a league whose players are mostly black—and whose fans and corporate sponsors who are mainly white."

The "racist" undergirdings of the "pearl drop strategy," however, offer an anachronistic racial dichotomy. This is because, in the post-Jordan era, race emerges in an internationalized NBA not only in a strictly bounded, black versus white sense. In the "phantom calls," race is conceived as a concatenation of political effects. It demands the linking together of different histories, continents, economies, cultures— American, African-American, Asian—in their always complicated relation to basketball, discourses about the body in public, and the nation itself. *Phantom Calls* explores the difficult, contorted, and fluid interplay of blackness, whiteness, and Asian-ness in relation to Yao Ming and the racial politics of the NBA. The focus in this pamphlet is on how these tensions, perceptions, and articulations of race mutate in their relationships to each other. In the terms suggested here, race can only be thought, in this moment of largely unhindered capital flows, as a phantasmatically complex logic. Race and racism are composed, in uneven degrees, of globalization, ethnicity, a complicated anti-Americanism, the reemergence of earlier, resolute and still efficacious articulations of (African-American) racial consciousness, and difficult translations from one national context to another.

In this era of globalization, the Phantom of race is articulated not through the body of the NBA's black (African-American) majority, but in the event of the minority athlete, who is not white but Asian. "Asian-ness" has often located Asian Americans outside of African-American blackness, which is to say, "above" African Americans in the racial economy. While Asians have never been fully absorbed into the paradigm of whiteness, they enjoy a proximity to whiteness as a "model minority" that is forever beyond the reach of African Americans. There are, in fact, cultural moments and modalities that make Asians and Asian Americans, sometimes temporarily, sometimes more permanently, indistinct from whites and whiteness.

It is this linking together of historical forces that preoccupies *Phantom Calls* here—how the effects of race emanate from the political locale that is the NBA, a space in which the once dominant back vs. white racial dialectic has now transmuted into the post-racial era that is proving to be anything but post-racial. Indeed, the politics of the NBA is once again fraught with the ghostly presence of race, now refracted through the Asian body. It is striking that what is revealed through the event of Yao is the politically familiar. What is familiar to the American political landscape is made available and re-encountered through what is putatively strange: the body of the Chinese athlete. Except, of course, that the "strange" Asian body has for over a Naismithian century been conceptually intimate with, if physically removed from, American basketball. In this respect, Yao is less the stranger amongst us than a distant athletic relative "returned," from afar, to bring to life repressed political and cultural Phantoms.

Articulated through the event of Yao, race emerges in *Phantom Calls* not only as a critique of globalization, but refigured as a discourse about the body and cultural history of the (Chinese) nation in the era of neo-liberalization. Yao evokes a series of dialectics between China and the West. Embedded in this dialectic is the ghostly discourse of physiological inferiority: the historical sense that Asia has been, that it can still be, overwhelmed by the stronger, "superior," Western body (with an especial anxiety about the athletic prowess of the black body). This unease is revealed by Yao as he reflects upon his own singularity as an NBA player. From the moment he was chosen as the number one pick by the Houston Rockets in 2002, Yao understood how he would have to bear the burden of cultural and historical over-representation for Asians and Asian Americans: "diving, gymnastics, table tennis. We've always been good at those sports. Not basketball. It's a Western sport, and we've never been good at it. So it means much more to China to have a star in basketball, because it says that in at least one way we can compete with the West. That's something China has not believed in a long time."

What is confronted in China is a unique historical phenomenon. It represents the coming-into-dominance of the neo-liberal Asian nation that is struggling, as much in full view of the world as privately, with the process of transition; a process for which it has been critiqued both internationally and locally. China is coming to terms with the changes that have taken place since the Cultural Revolution—the adoption of a market economy under Communist Party (CP) rule, a single party domination that has seen many challenges to its authority, especially the event of Tiananmen Square in June 1989. China manifests itself as fully located in a moment of intense contradictions: a neo-liberal capitalist economy overseen by a CP that favors "open markets" but not, in

Karl Popper's terms, an "open society." China is now "capitalist" without being democratic, a nominally socialist society without anything remotely like a planned economy. Deeply suspicious of the West, it has in the past decade become the biggest beneficiary of direct foreign investment by Western capital. Whereas it was, during the Cultural Revolution, strongly opposed to organized sport (because it glorified the individual), it has since its readmission to the Olympic movement in 1979 aggressively pursued medals. China has been investing large amounts of money in the national sports system, an athletic model inherited from its old socialist comrades, the Soviet Union.

Son of the "Whore of Asia"

> Within a year, Mao's peasant army swept their way
> into Shanghai, and the complacent foreigners who
> had whiled away their leisure hours at the Country
> Club fled. China's puritanical new rulers, appalled
> by the capitalist excesses that had turned Shanghai
> into the "Whore of Asia," seized all of the city's
> clubs as part of their strategy to suffocate the
> former center of "bourgeois influence."
>
> Brooks Larmer, *Operation Yao Ming*

Born in September 1980, Yao is the son of two
basketball players. His father, Yao Zhiyuan, was only
a journeyman, but his mother, Fang Feng Di,
captained the Chinese women's team to the gold
medal in the 1976 Asian Games. (His parents are
known, colloquially, as "Da Yao" and "Da Fang,"
"Big Yao" and "Big Fang.") Fang's gold medal was
especially important because it came in basketball,
one of what the Chinese call the "big ball" sports.
After graduating through the nation's basketball
system, Yao joined his hometown Shanghai Sharks.
He helped them win the Chinese Basketball
Association (CBA) championship in 2002, after three
consecutive championship losses to the People's
Liberation Army (PLA) team, the Bayi Rockets. The
Bayi team is Beijing-based, and was anchored by
Yao's keenest rival, the center Wang Zhizhi—himself
a star player.

Drafted by the Dallas Mavericks in 1999,
Wang only joined the NBA franchise in April 2001

because the CBA did not want to lose their premier player to the US. From China to the US, back across the Pacific, from the CBA to the NBA, Wang and Yao's careers have cast ghostly shadows over each other. (During their days on the Chinese national team, Wang, Yao, and Mengke Bateer, the three centers, dubbed themselves the "Great Wall of China.") Three years younger than his arch-rival, Yao acknowledged that "Wang gave me this new idea of what I could become." And, as things turned out, an even keener idea of what he could not be. Part of the reason for the tense relationship between Yao and Wang is because they represent different images of China. As a lieutenant in the PLA, playing for the military's Bayi team, and located in Beijing, Wang was—before his precipitous fall—the unsmiling face of the CP's central authority. Before his departure to the US, Wang's Bayi dominated the CBA.

As a Shanghai native, Yao's status, on the other hand, can be said to derive from the city's cosmopolitan, modern status. At the turn of the twentieth century, Shanghai ranked amongst the world's most important cities. This standing has now, at the beginning of the new millennium, been partially recovered. Dubbed the "Paris of the Orient" during the colonial era, Shanghai was a city at the hub of China's cultural and commercial exchange with Asia and the West. It was, however, precisely this proximity to Western modernity that made it susceptible to severe restrictions by the CP from 1949 to 1990, when its second economic and cultural renaissance began in earnest. Condemned for its parasitic role as a colonial treaty port, Shanghai was known during that era as the "Whore of Asia."

This moniker might, then, explain a key element of the city's illicit folklore. Renowned in China not only for its arrogance (its residents are said to be more disliked by their compatriots than people from any other region), the Shanghainese are on average noticeably taller than Chinese from other regions. The reason for this quite visible physical discrepancy, the underground story goes, is the pre-Liberation sex worker industry that, presumably, produced several offspring with non-Chinese fathers. Celebrated as he is by his fellow-Chinese and the national sports authority alike for his height, Yao's loftiness—if one follows the logic of the city's illicit history—comes genetically not from China but somewhere else. Yao's height can be attributed to the ghosts of a libidinous Shanghai time that has passed and, like all ghosts, is now returning with the city's second rise to economic and cultural prominence. Today Western tourists to Shanghai go in search of those vestiges of the city's grand architectural past. The old Shanghai, with its colonial buildings and lush, meticulously designed gardens, is what these visitors want to see.

There is also a more contemporary version of that architectural ghost. After the massive collapse of the Asian economies in 1997, many of Shanghai's new high rises, built to house a growing middle class, were left either uncompleted or empty—the would-be tenants unable to afford the cost of accommodation in glitzy skyscrapers. Those high rises came to constitute their own "ghost towns," either abandoned entirely or taken over by immigrants from the rural areas unable to pay for housing in the city; they were only too happy to take up residence in the uninhabited, frequently incomplete skyscrapers. In both respects, Shanghai is a city haunted by its long-ago and more recent past.

Shanghainese folklore contrasts with a more conspiratorial theory about Yao's extraordinary height, a theory that extends to Wang and relies upon a genealogical rather than libidinal historical account. In *Operation Yao Ming*, Larmer argues that Yao and Wang are the freakishly tall products of a "genetic conspiracy." "Since the 1950s," Larmer writes, "the sports system has brought together the nation's tallest people into a controlled environment, provided them with nourishment and training, fostered their intermarriage and procreation, and culled their tallest and most talented offspring to become basketball players themselves." Like Yao, Wang's parents, Wang Weijun and Ren Huanzhen, were basketball players, good enough to be active in the national sports programs. Da Fang and Ren, in fact, played against each other during their careers. By all accounts, Ren was the more talented player. Fang, critics argue, owed her career to her intense loyalty to the Cultural Revolution. Yao's mother is remembered as a "belligerent Red Guard," a ruthless stormtrooper of and for Mao's vision of a socialist China.

The veracity of Larmer's claims rests upon, it would seem, fairly solid "genetic" (basketball) grounds. The scientific evidence, especially in a society as closed as China's, may be harder to find. So rumors of "growth hormone therapy" remain just that: unfounded but growing speculation about China as the "new East Germany." One can only await the 2008 Beijing Olympics, already widely figured as Yao's PR coming out party, with real trepidation. The promise of drug scandals, doping, and the pressure on officials and judges could make 2008 an Olympics like no other. When, as expected, Yao leads the Chinese team out for the opening ceremonies, all eyes will be on him not only as the tallest flag bearer, but the new face of China. Or, the face of the new China.

The "legacy" system implemented by the Chinese basketball authorities, in which the offspring of basketball players are privileged by virtue of their athletic lineage rather than the merits of their talents, enabled the officials to function as de facto marriage counselors who anticipated very tall fringe benefits from their charges' extracurricular activities. Even this way, however, the Shanghainese had an advantage. Being taller than average to begin with, players from the region were likely to produce "big." Yao was thus geographically predisposed to triumph over Wang. Fang's son was always going to be taller than her old rival, Ren's—even if Yao was initially the more reluctant player. So being the son of the Dengite "Whore of Asia" is good for a great deal of height, fame, and access to exactly the kind of foreign capital that earned Shanghai its derogatory moniker in the first place.

The Phantom Calls

As professional leagues, the NBA and the CBA are so far apart that one could argue they administer different sports. The CBA is static, unimaginative, light years slower, and largely devoid of the kind of physical contact that is routine in the NBA. In the NBA the guards are quick and immensely creative, the forwards are fast and powerful and capable of making shots from almost anywhere on the court. Most players defend with conviction. There is, however, no position that is as physically demanding as the center spot. Mikan, Russell, and Abdul-Jabbar set the standard for defensive toughness. In the 1980s, Malone, Ewing, and Olajuwon, and in the 1990s, David Robinson and

Shaquille O'Neal, each added their own wrinkles to the tradition of hardnosed defending. The center position has always been premised on dominant "paint play:" rough and tumble exchanges that take place in the most combative zone in basketball, underneath the basket where players jostle, elbow each other, grab, and push. This is the no-holds-barred region, where players scrap for rebounds, "tip-ins" (scoring an "easy bucket"), second shots, and any form of an extra possession.

Yao came into the league as a different kind of center. A good shot blocker because of his height, technique, and anticipation, he showed a real dislike for the more rigorous demands of "paint play." Yao certainly grabs his fair share of NBA rebounds (as well as blocking a significant number of shots), but his favored method of scoring is from the perimeter. With his much admired "feathery" shooting touch, he's a good outside shooter—a skill normally attributed more to a small forward or a guard than to a center. He is not, as they say in the NBA, a "post-up" man, demanding the ball (often with the center's back turned to the basket) where the physicality is at its most intense. The word quickly got around in the NBA: Yao is "soft." Not the reputation a franchise center wants to have.

For foreign players entering the NBA, the physicality of the league arguably requires the biggest adjustment. This is especially true for the game's "big men"—the forwards and the centers. Guards, from Croatia's Drazen Petrovic and Tony Kukoc to France's Tony Parker, find the process of adapting easier, in part because they do not have to endure as much physical punishment as the "big men." It is also true that those foreign recruits who have played in US colleges have less trouble adjusting to the demands of the NBA game. (To date, only one Chinese player, Ma Jian, has played Division I basketball in the NCAA. He did not, despite trying out with a few NBA teams, get picked up.) Jamaican-born Ewing, Nigerian-born Olajuwon, Congolese-born Dikembe Mutombo, and the US Virgin Islands-born Tim Duncan, are all players who thrived—and still do, in Duncan's case—in the NBA. (The ageing Mutombo is currently the back-up center to Yao in Houston.) These players are prepared for the rigors of the NBA game that their European counterparts are not. Germany's Detlef Schrempf and the Netherlands' Rik Smits, while successful in the league, did not have either the "post-up" presence or the longevity of a Ewing. Like Yao, Smits and Schrempf had good outside games, but neither were renowned for their inside presence. As much as players like Yao or Kukoc struggle with the intense physicality and defensive demands of the NBA, so different from the less robust CBA or the more offensive-minded European leagues, the NBA remains the desired locale in international basketball. It is the league, and not only because its players are the best remunerated, with the greatest opportunities for endorsements. The NBA is the standard against which all players, from Asia to Australia, want to measure themselves.

If the NBA regular season contests (82 games, half at home, half on the road) are hard fought, they are nothing compared to the brutal competitiveness of the playoffs. As a player with a less than desirable physical "rep," the playoffs were yet another testing ground for Yao. His passing and his perimeter shooting make him an unconventional threat for opposing centers. However, the NBA playoffs turn on a combination of skill and a desire to win, all of it grounded in a willingness to play tough ball for 48 minutes. In the playoffs, NBA insiders say, the competitors "step up" their game.

The 2004-05 playoffs, Yao's first, were for him a whole new basketball universe. He played decently, rebounding, passing, and knocking down some big shots. But during the series against the Dallas Mavericks, Yao—according to Van Gundy—found himself falling foul of the referees with a certain regularity. Yao was whistled on both the offensive and defensive ends of the court. When Houston had the ball, he was called for setting moving screens—moving his body to obstruct opponents, thereby illegally "freeing up" his teammates; on defense, Yao was called for going over the back and for reaching in, which are against the rules of the game. As the all-Texas series wore on, Van Gundy and Yao became more and more frustrated with the officiating.

After a dispiriting loss in Game 5, in which the Mavs pushed the Rockets, down 3-2, to the brink of elimination, Van Gundy exploded at the referees. (Yao played really well in this game, scoring 30 points.) Van Gundy charged that Yao was the victim of "phantom calls," creating great consternation amongst NBA referees and administrators alike. The real foul, according to Van Gundy, was committed against Yao rather than by him. It was not Yao who was breaking the rules, but the officials who were "errant" in their decisions. Van Gundy had been complaining for a couple of seasons about the officiating against his Chinese star. The issue came to a boil in the Mavericks series when the Dallas owner, the irrepressibly self-promoting and widely disliked Mark Cuban, sent tapes of Yao's "offences" to the NBA office. Infuriated by Cuban's actions, Van Gundy claimed that a "referee and longtime friend, who was not working the playoffs... told him that the league office was instructing referees to pay particular attention to Yao's moving screens." Van Gundy was fined $100,000—the most severe penalty imposed upon a coach in the history of the NBA. Ever the loyal team player, Yao offered to split the fine with his coach. It remains unclear whether that financial burden was indeed equally borne by coach and player, but the gesture was wonderfully Yaoesque. Loyalty to the team, as we will see, is fundamental to Yao's approach. Yao was prepared to "take one for the team," even if, as was later disclosed, NBA rules forbade such a gesture.

The referees' "phantom calls" unleashed a racial politics that was foreclosed during the rhetorical skirmishes that erupted around the "fouled" Asian body. The Asian body had, Van Gundy implied, been done an injustice precisely because it was an Asian and not a black body. The "phantom calls" reveal a series of linked paradoxes: Yao's body was vulnerable to "unfair" calls because it was, like the white body, a minority in a league dominated by blacks, a constituency that was, outside the lines of the court, itself a political minority. According to the writer David Shields, these paradoxes constitute their own kind of racial justice. The circumscribed privileges black NBA athletes enjoy, Shields argues in the provocatively entitled *Black Planet*, represent a kind of "racial payback:"

> Nearly all the head coaches are white; nearly all the refs are white; nearly all the fans are white; nearly all the broadcasters are white (except for former players, who serve as "color commentators"); nearly all the owners are white. The players are the de facto owners; the coaches are the de facto slaves; it's the history of the country turned upside down.

I don't think the NBA is the "history of the country turned upside down," but it is, as Shields indicates, a particularized universe in which Yao is "racially disenfranchised." Black centers such as Shaq and Duncan enjoy a status not afforded to Yao. Whether or not that gets them and not Yao the calls is a debatable matter. However, Van Gundy was doing his best to suggest that the "de facto" owners be reined in, more than just a little. It is a measure of the racial economy of the NBA that, in this new allotment of roles, it is the Asian and not the African-American athlete who has to bear the burden of vulnerability. Or, as several Asian-American commentators have said, race is now located as an explosive politics in the yellow body. The black body remains raced, but a different kind of politics, a different kind of social disruption, emanates from it. In the modality of the NBA's globalization it is historically telling that Yao Ming, model representative of neo-liberal China, catalyzes a return to the discourse of race. (In Van Gundy's assessment, "If you were going to have an ambassador for your country in a sport, you couldn't find a better one than Yao Ming.") The event of the "phantom calls" marks, definitively, the end of the post-racial Jordan discourse.

The Jordan years, characterized as they were by the massive expansion of capitalism in the NBA, were premised on the transcendence of race. However, even in the imagined post-racial Jordan age, blackness was present as a transgressive, oppositional mode. Players such as Dennis Rodman, him of the theatrical, self-aggrandizing self-representation, and Latrell Sprewell, who once choked his coach when he was playing for the Golden State Warriors, and Rasheed Wallace, who has a talent for drawing fouls for "over-aggressive" play and excessive talking back to referees, provided a counterpoint to the "civility" of Jordan. In the current era there is Ron Artest, a brilliant defender known as an extremely combative malcontent, and Allen "AI" Iverson, the NBA's much-ballyhooed "bad boy." All of these players, each in their own way, have used their bodies, their on-court demeanor, and their off-court activities, to mark race as indefatigably constitutive of the NBA, no matter the public presentation of Jordan and the efforts of Stern's PR company to the contrary. Nevertheless, Jordan's was an era in which race was never publicly an issue in the NBA.

Phantom Calls is, for this reason, not simply about explicating how, despite its elliptical presence, its silencing, and its political non-speaking, race was constitutive of the Yao event. The calls mark the reconfiguration of race as a political category in the new NBA. The calls made against Yao Ming, and Van Gundy's invocation of the Phantom, have now made imperative the very discussion that Jordan-era NBA players avoided, ignored, or glibly glossed over—a discussion also invoked in the current era as a "moral" critique of the "bad boys." One of Jordan's great competitors, the brash Charles Barkley, may have summed up the ethos of the era best with his unrepentant Nike ad: "I am not a role model." Barkley's proclamation was a crude code for the star's refusal to represent African Americans; it was also an assertion of his unrestricted right to capital accumulation, unimpeded by the demands of racial affiliation or a commitment to social justice of either the local or global variety.

Barkley was no more against the degradation of the African-American inner city than he was opposed to the working conditions in Nike sweatshops in Southeast Asia. In the epigrammatic slogan for his ad, "I am not a role model," Barkley was dismissing race entirely. He was speaking against the Phantoms who haunted his own cultural heritage, that tradition that did not disavow race. With his signature hubris, Barkley was grandstanding against the struggles and accomplishments of his league's predecessors, together with such iconic figures as Jackie Robinson and Muhammad Ali. These were athletes who took seriously their status as African Americans at odds with the American way. These were athletes who understood their role in the race wars that surrounded them, and what the political consequences of their positions were. It is not only that Barkley knew what he was—a late-capitalist entrepreneur thriving in and because of the NBA— but that he also knew what he did not want to be: a man defined by race. In tacitly discounting race and by distancing themselves from any and all forms of social injustice, Barkley and Jordan were, of course, also disengaging from any critique of the racism foundational to American society. Jackie Robinson had offered his criticisms implicitly, almost always marked by his trademark restraint; Ali and American football star Jim Brown were defiantly public in their denunciations of American racism. In a perverse way, Barkley's disavowal of race in the 1990s was only possible because of what Robinson and Ali and Brown had done, and, in Ali's case, so poetically, defiantly, said. It was precisely Barkley's contextual majority that relieved him of the burden of race.

More than the reanimation of race as a critical category within the NBA, for African Americans as well as the Asian subject, the "phantom calls" also reveal race as a category complicated by the mobility of labor in the age of global capital. Through Yao's body, race is reconstructed as an anti-imperial category with significant consequences for the local (USA; NBA) discourse about race and racism. It is in his Shanghainese origins that Yao is able to make evident how race—even in so rarefied a site of labor as the

NBA court—can return to haunt the US as the privileged, lucrative location of culture. It is because of his status as non-American that Yao makes clear how race and globalization are constitutive of each other across historical time and space. Because globalization renders national boundaries porous, it has made possible the event of a Shanghai basketball player who insists on a different racial consciousness as a full-blown discussion about race in the United States. Yao's status as raced subject produces a conception of race and racism simultaneously in conversation with and in excess of America.

Yao's conception of racism, addressed as it is to the US, is premised on the notion that, as he says, racism "is not a problem in China." "First of all," he explains, "...almost everybody is of the same race. There are fifty-five minorities in China, but they are very small." Spoken like a true member of the Han majority. While 93% of all Chinese are Han, Yao does not even spare a thought here for his national teammate Bateer, an Inner Mongolian. By insisting that "racism is not a problem in China," Yao is not suggesting that there is no awareness of racism in his country. On the contrary, he is historically conscious of it as a practice that has been eliminated in China. As he says prosaically in his autobiography, *Two Worlds*, "We are taught in school that a long time ago there was racism, but it ended with the Communist liberation in 1949." Never, apparently, to raise its ugly head again. Declared dead by decree, it did not reemerge in another form after Mao came to power. Even the situation in Tibet, where nationality and ethnicity (if not race) are powerfully linked, is dismissed as a Western concern by Yao: "Tibet is another topic that I feel is more talked about in the US than in China. Most Chinese people think that Tibet has been part of China for a very long time. If a Chinese president were to allow Tibet to go free, I suspect that would be remembered in China as a big sin." For Yao, an independent Tibet is nothing but a Western "fantasy," yet another failure by the colonial-ists and neo-colonialists to respect China's "extensive" sovereignty. The situation in Xianjang, where nation-alist fervor is equally strong, does not even merit a mention by Yao.

Historicizing racism, fixing it in and as the past, is a deft rhetorical maneuver by Yao. It is his way of displacing it entirely to the US, suggesting that discriminatory practices are alien to China, that racism is an American discourse and problem. And yet, in explaining why the African-American agent Bill Duffy—Yao's US agent—had to be kept out of sight during the process of negotiating Yao's release to the NBA, Larmer argues otherwise, and pulls no punches: "What patriotic Chinese official would leave Yao's safekeeping in the hands of an American, and a black one at that, given China's barely concealed racist tendencies?" Lest we imagine that this is simply Larmer's American racial consciousness at work, Yao himself reveals the Darwinian tropes sometimes oper-ative in Chinese racial discourse. After his 1998 trip to the US for a series of summer basketball camps, Yao remembers: "All of our teammates called us 'black monkeys' because we had gotten so tan in America."

When it comes to racism, neither China nor Yao's thinking has, despite Mao's best "Cultural" efforts, absorbed fully the lessons of the 1949 Revolution.

However, despite Yao's unconvincing disavowal, there is in his engagement a greater public articulation than Jordan ever offered. It is not simply that the event of Yao produces a discourse about race, but that Yao himself addresses the issue of racism. For all his global ubiquity and transnational symbolism (or, perhaps, because of it), Jordan remained not only silent on matters of racial or economic injustice but locked into parochialism—a "national" provinciality. Like Barkley, Jordan never spoke out against the sweatshops in Asia that made the Nike Air Jordan sneakers from which he profited so royally. Jordan's was a virtual cosmopolitanism; he was less an actual traveler to foreign countries than an image replicated from one country's collection of billboards to another. His Airness was a global technological presence. While Jordan remained unreflective in his hegemonic American-ness, this privilege has not ever been available to Yao.

The Shanghainese center understands fully what his status as Chinese basketballer in the West signifies in his native country, where all of his games are broadcast (courtesy of NBA) to the nation. "The way I think about it," Yao says, "it's a great honor to represent China to the outside world." To represent China, that is, in America, from whence all self-representations that have truly global desires flow. Hailing from without, disrupting the within of his hosts, Yao releases into global political play more

Phantoms, surely, than the intrepid Van Gundy could have imagined when he protested those fouls. Contrary to what many commentators suggested, there was more than the integrity of NBA officiating at stake because of the "phantom calls" that plagued Yao in the playoff series against the Mavericks. The very processes of racialized globalization were laid open to scrutiny.

Who Can Speak Race?

Murder most foul, as in the best it is,
But this most foul, strange and unnatural.
                    Shakespeare, *Hamlet*, Act I Sc V.

As this critique of Yao and Van Gundy's comments shows, there is no time of race that is not also, invariably, the articulation of other racisms. The enunciation of race as it applies to the event at hand is always more than the racism of the contemporary conjuncture; it always exceeds the particularities and generalities of this time and place. In this way, race and racism are always in excess of, more than, and constitutively outside of, themselves. Racism can never, for this reason, fully know itself or explain itself to itself; it is salient, then, that it is, in distinct moments, able to speak as itself. Because it does not, and will never, fully know itself, racism can never know precisely when or how it will speak itself. It is, for this reason, primarily in its discursive excessiveness that racism can be heard to speak as itself, sometimes unknowingly, often as a contradiction. The contradictory, contingent nature of racial articulation can be identified in those moments when the figure of discursive initiation (here, Van Gundy) speaks from a disjunctive—or, non-raced—place, as in those racist Phantoms released into public circulation in sites where their presence and articulation are not expected. Or, when one instance of racism inadvertently illuminates or draws attention to another, apparently discrete racism, that has for a while lain dormant, as when the yellow body is concatenated with the black body.

As a white coach, renowned for his loyalty to his tough African-American players, Van Gundy understood the discursive parameters in which he was operating. (Among his favorite players for the New York Knicks, whom he used to coach, was Ewing, currently his assistant at the Rockets with a special responsibility for the development of Yao.) Visibly angered by the phantom calls—"I challenge them to say Yao is refereed appropriately"—Van Gundy went on to choose his words carefully in his critique of the NBA referees: "Nobody wants to use the word 'bias.' It sets people off. You have to be careful." Hence Van Gundy's designation of the fouls called against Yao as "phantoms." The coach will not name it "discrimination" or a "miscarriage of justice." That is because the phantasm, race and racism, is the enunciation of that which is most feared, that which is most determinedly and deeply repressed. The Phantom, Van Gundy recognizes, can radically disrupt the socio-economic and political functioning of the present. The Phantom is that which must, even though it requires considerable effort, not be allowed public speaking because it represents an a-temporality that is profoundly historical. The threat of disarticulation, the unmaking of the present dispensation by historical forces originating and operative in the past, always inheres in the Phantom. Even as it is dormant in the present, the Phantom's potential for reemergence is such that it must always be guarded against, always be anticipated with dread, always regarded as a threat to the precarious ground upon which the present rests. (Such as the Jordan era was always mildly haunted by Rodman's antics and Sprewell's anger; such as the current NBA is perpetually uneasy about AI's "gansta," hip-hop persona.) In temporal terms, the Phantom is never gone; it is always phantasmatically contemporary and it is always, forebodingly, visible on the political and cultural horizon—as the path from Rodman through Sprewell to Iverson. As constitutive as it is of the past, so it shadows the future as a peculiarly unrelenting threat.

The Phantom's capacity for transcendence is what makes it the very opposite of that which is not presumed to be real. The Phantom is all too real because it is historically manifest: it has a history that stretches all the way into the past and it casts a long shadow over the future. Those calls, those fouls of which Yao is potentially guilty, and therefore also potentially innocent, constitute the act of a phantasmatic calling out that releases into political consequence the racialized history of the NBA and, more importantly, the United States. The calling out that Van Gundy engages in represents a protest against the injustice inflicted upon Yao that echoes other historical wrongs committed against (differently) raced bodies. The "phantom calls," the "fouls" that were not fouls, according to the white coach, stand in as a name for that injustice whose proper political designation is race and racism. This history that is contained within that name allows, through Van Gundy's utterance, the symbolic recollection of the racist un-conscious that has defined American society; an unconscious, moreover, that is particularly now back in play in the NBA.

As Shakespeare might have it, there is in the phantom calls a "history most foul." A history that includes, but is not limited to, those barred from playing in the white leagues and the routine Jim Crow discrimination endured by the Globetrotters and the Rens. In this archive of racial history we learn of segregation, inferior facilities, and racism as experienced by black players in the NBA's early and middle years; we learn also of the symbolic whiteness that defined the era of the "Celtics mystique," despite Russell's towering presence. There are also the endorsement opportunities denied model NBA citizens—such as Oscar Robertson, the 1960s star of the Cincinnati Royals— simply because they were African Americans.

There is in the phantasmatic call a long history of racism in American sport. A history that goes back to the boxer Jack Johnson, the Olympic athletes Jesse Owens and Wilma Rudolph, and the tennis stars Althea Gibson and Arthur Ashe. A history, in other words, that goes back beyond the first black NBA players; a narrative that precedes the moment of Jackie Robinson and Larry Doby (the first black player in the American League). The real phantasmatic of Van Gundy's call, crossing and making alliances across racial lines and vast geographical boundaries as it does, is only partially audible in the political violence of antebellum America. It is only partially discernible in the dynamic energies and commitments of the Civil Rights movement, and in the poetic stridency of the Black Arts Movement and the 1960s black nationalism of Malcolm X, Huey Newton, and Angela Davis. But within the larger cultural imaginary of black America, there may be other locales where the phantasmatic is more resonantly, yet subtly, audible.

The Phantom can be heard in the Southern-saturated blues of Robert Johnson, in the surprisingly unsettling melodies of Louis "Satchmo" Armstrong, in the plaintive wailing of Billie Holiday, and the choppy modernist phrasings of Charlie Parker and Miles Davis. The Phantom is ominously present in the quiet, dark protagonists who people William Faulkner's South, those black characters who move mostly unseen and unacknowledged among the dysfunctional, incestuous white folk; the phantasmatic is detectable in the thwarted dreams of Ralph Ellison's black sharecroppers as much as in the terrible, illuminating fate that is his main character's "invisibility"—after all, what is the Phantom if not the reconfiguration of the "spook" in *Invisible Man*? The ghost is painfully "afoot," like the restless spirit of dead King Hamlet, in religion, politics and sexuality; in James Baldwin's fiction, it haunts blackness, sometimes to the point of making Baldwin's protagonists choose "another country." The title of a famous Baldwin novel, *Another Country*, serves as a trope for suicide as much as a metaphor for the excruciatingly painful pleasures of exile. In the literature of our moment, the Phantom is uncannily active in the suppressed longings of Toni Morrison's women who live, among other addresses, on the Bluestone Road of *Beloved*. "124 Bluestone Road was haunted," goes the novel's opening line, locating us immediately in the ghostly presence of antebellum America. In *Paradise*, a later work, the "convent" at the edge of the all-black town proves to be little more than a transient haven, only momentarily a "paradise." In these literary texts, as much as in the history of race and racism in American sport and culture, there is the ghostly presence of race: the past that is not yet, will never be, passed; the past that is unfailingly expected to manifest itself again and again in the future.

Van Gundy's protest about the phantasmatic releases ambivalence, uncertainty, and controversy into the racial politics of the NBA. Controversy, as league watchers know, is an aspect of NBA life that the unfortunately named Commissioner Stern most intensely abhors. For Stern only two modes are acceptable for the NBA: infinite capital expansion and socio-political equilibrium while doing so. According to his critics, Stern has always grasped the root law of capitalism: "grow or die." Anything that disrupts the NBA's (international) growth or invites critical media attention is unwelcome and subject to discipline. Through naming the unspeakable without its proper naming, the Phantom introduces the politics of contingency: an indefatigable uncertainty, a series of disconcerting possibilities.

Van Gundy was, as the hefty fine levied by Stern testifies, taking a substantial risk in raising the specter of racism—even if he can only go so far as (not) to name it "bias." In making the critique, Van Gundy raised many questions, not least about his own motivations: Was Van Gundy simply attempting to protect his player from the referees, as any good coach would do? Was the loaded invocation of the Phantom designed to counteract Mark Cuban's questionable actions? Was the Phantom an appropriate naming because it raised the specter of race while maintaining, for Yao, the "exemplary" Asian player, a critical distance from blackness? In the evocation of the "phantom calls," race and racism raise themselves precisely as a disruptive contingency, as the opportunity to provoke political suspicion about the white speaker and the subject of race; and, to a lesser extent, about the "integrity" of NBA refereeing and the administering of the league itself. This political uncertainty allows for speculation about justice and injustice, about the fairness of the referees, about how "bias" might or might not be a contributing factor to the vulnerability of the raced body, the raced Asian body that is vulnerable because of its diasporic location.

However, once the contingency has been publicly uttered it immediately proceeds beyond itself. The contingency assumes, so to speak, the hue of certainty as soon as it starts to circulate through repetition: it represents only momentarily a hesitation, an articulation seeking its own epistemological footing, because it rapidly comes to constitute through its speaking—as it is disseminated widely—the political ground of race and racism that it was, for that brief instant of uncertainty, only gesturing toward. The politics and history of the Phantom replaces "bias" with its proper name, "racism." And in this case it forces upon us a more demanding question: is the Phantom of racism against blacks the same as the one against Asians? How are these Phantoms either linked or disjunctive with each other? In this instance, the contingency is the foundation upon which the politics of race rests.

In the controversial echoes of the Van Gundy contretemps is the articulation of counter-calls, narratives that encode histories of oppositionality, marginality, and difference—that litany of injustices enumerated earlier. In the act of calling "foul," there is revealed the distinguished history of "calling against" that is integral to the genetic makeup of the Phantom. Included in that history is Russell's (and, later, K.C. Jones's) racial salience in Boston, Wilt's flashy moves in Philadelphia and Los Angeles, Oscar Robertson's impeccable distribution skills in Cincinnati, Dr. J's lighting up of the Philly sky, and Elgin Baylor's and later Magic's scintillating tenures in Los Angeles. For all these players, and several others, the act of "calling against" was not only constituted out of their racial difference, but articulated in their innovativeness—their capacity to change the game. These players made it, through their flair, skill, and exquisite sense of moment, an entirely different game from that which Naismith had invented. Not for these African-American players the "invisibility" of a Clifton or Lloyd. While they may be either forgotten or on the threshold of erasure, they were all determined to make themselves as "unforgettable" as a smooth Nat King Cole ballad; in part, perhaps, because they too were haunted by those, like Cooper, who had been too quickly forgotten. So even as they are forgotten, or stand in danger of being forgotten, Jordan's predecessors are hauntingly—like a friendly ghost, this time—present in his transcendence. His unique moves, such as that famed fall-away jumper, his unbelievable "hang time," contain within them the history of other moves. How could Jordan have conceived of "hang time" without the cultural memory of Dr. J? How could Ewing have defended so stoutly for years without the bustling presence in his game of a Russell or a Willis Reed? Within the racialized history of the NBA, there is always "something afoot," some other time in play, something other at work than what is being executed and observed now; a time, a history, now stretched by globalization, now linked by capitalist expansion, to other places.

The history of the NBA is, in this way, very much like King Hamlet's ghost. What is instructive about Shakespeare's dead sovereign is his capacity to spectralize his demise, making it impossible for the "murder most foul" to be forgotten, for the life of Claudius's court to continue as though it were a time unto itself, disconnected from other historical moments. The departed king's ghost disrupts so that it cannot be passed over in death. The dead ghost protects against a menace far greater than its own "unnatural" death. There is at the core of the racist phantasmatic an unthinkable violence: the elimination of an entire people. It is the task of the Phantom, in its several returns, rearticulations, and reanimations, to work against the phantasmatic nightmare. At its most reductive level, the natural disasters of December 2004 and September 2005 made this abundantly clear. Raced populations victimized by the Asian tsunami (from Sri Lanka to Indonesia) and Hurricane Katrina (that ravaged the predominantly black city of New Orleans) are not only surplus to the demands of capital; labor no longer required by the demands of postmodern technology, they are literally expendable. They can, in full view of the world's cameras, be left to die because they have no use. King Hamlet's death may indeed have been "unnatural," but in the new century natural forces work as well as "unnatural" ones against those who can be, must be, disposed of biopolitically. The racist phantasmatic—the racist unconscious—articulates itself in, as Shakespeare might have it, chillingly "strange" and unimaginably violent ways. Death through indifference: that is what the Phantom militates against in its continual return, in its refusal to go quietly.

Race is the ghost that Stern imagined Jordan had finally buried. As things turned out, it was nothing but a temporary respite. That race returned is not surprising, though the Houston-via-Shanghai guise in which it reemerged certainly caught many post-racialists napping. The Phantom's reentry into NBA life can be attributed to its infinite creativity, the unexpected forms it can assume (a 7'6" Shanghai center), and the mutations into which it can insinuate itself. What is truly significant about the Yao event is not the ubiquity and permeability of racism. It is, rather, its ostensible out of placeness: during the NBA playoffs, within the comfy confines of the basketball court, in the putative moment of the post-racial NBA subject.

Racism is, in this context and, moreover, in this moment, to invoke another metaphor from Shakespeare, "out of joint" with the times. In the post-Jordan, globalized NBA, race is not supposed to take

on these Asian guises, race is not supposed to
announce itself—even when it is only designated
"bias"—so vividly and so viscerally. The Yao event
demonstrates that the discourse of post-racialism in
the global age is the "true" fantasy, the unreal imagin-
ings of those political constituencies who—even
though they may or may not know it—live in fear of
the Phantom and want to eliminate it from public
discourse. The blackness that Jordan never owned,
that His Airness supposedly disposed of, is refracted
through Yao's "yellowness." It is paradoxical, then,
that the non-native Asian reveals the depths of the
racial problematic within. The unenviable American
familiar, the history of race and racism, must not be
allowed to return in the figure of the strange—the
figure of the strange must not be permitted to make
public the superficiality and unsustainability of the
post-racial fantasy.

Through the process of post-raciliazing or de-
raciliazing the NBA, the effect is not to de-race but to
re-racialize: negating the negation creates the neces-
sity for a new name, "bias," that is inextricably linked
to that other name, racism. Like the ghost of
Shakespeare's dead King, the event of the athletic
body—at rest or in motion, whether it is setting "ille-
gal" screens or picking up unjust "fouls"—can never
go un-named. The event of the athletic body that is
not white—whether that body is African-American or
Asian, Latin American or European—is such that it
must always be properly designated politically. The
vulnerability of the Chinese center to questionable
"fouls" serves, in this way, as an unexpected riposte to

post-racialist discourse. It would be unreflective to dismiss post-racialism as the political "time that is out of joint," but the event of Yao certainly suggests that it is a discourse fermenting ideas that are, if not "rotten," by Shakespearean standards, then certainly of questionable use—and veracity.

By challenging the ideological tenor imposed on these unexpectedly unruly times, for America and the NBA in their different ways, the Phantom instantiates the politics of the contretemps. The Phantom is the inopportune occurrence, the embarrassing mischance, which erupts into—and thereby deconstructs and disrupts—the dominant political discourse. Ironic, then, that in his desire to capture the Chinese market Stern disturbed the ghosts he had worked so hard, à la *Hamlet*'s Claudius, to consign to history. A history, however, that revealed a larger, ghostly, trajectory, connecting Yao to Naismith, Shanghai to Houston; a history of basketball that reveals the basketball "Orient" to be, unlike in the colonialist account, a cultural condition that antecedes and does not lag behind the "West." Shanghai is prior to Houston in Naismith's scheme of things. The Commissioner may rule the NBA with a czarist hand, but he cannot, much as he would want, put the Phantom to rest. Instead, Stern's foray into China yielded Yao whose body raised a royal racial ruckus. The contretemps around race enabled a forceful going against, going counter to, the dominant thinking and in so doing makes possible another time of and for articulation—and possibly even several other temporalities.

Speaking For

> There was nothing in between
> no mediating look or word
> to conceal his wretchedness—or hers.
> > Milan Kundera, *Life is Elsewhere*

Race and racism, however, especially as they reference African Americans in relation to the event of Yao, are strange phenomena. Exactly how complicated and tendentious they are to speak is evident in the truncations, gaps, and silences that abound in Van Gundy's denunciations of the referees. By claiming prejudicial officiating against Yao, Van Gundy raises a specter that is disruptive to the post-racial, globalized representation of the NBA. Van Gundy's call compels more, however, than a globalized perspective, the recognition that the NBA now belongs in the world, with all its specialized, skilled gastarbeiters hailing from all over the world—even, of course, as the NBA is still primarily a US corporation. Van Gundy's silence about the local begins as a critique of the local and the ways in which that local both can and cannot accommodate Yao as a political subject. By positioning Yao as the symbolic victim of the American racial phantasmatic and his refusal to name race or racism, by "mediating" Yao, in Kundera's sense, Van Gundy makes possible a discussion about the condition of racial politics as it pertains to African-American players in the NBA. Van Gundy provokes one racialized question more than any other: Is Yao the target of "phantom calls" because he is not black? The condition of the NBA in its post-racial formation is such that the preponderance of African-American players has made it a cultural space that is "out of joint" with the rest of American society. Within the peculiar racial dynamic that is the NBA, the black player—at least since the demise of Bird's figuratively white Celtics in the late-1980s—is hegemonic and looks likely to be so for a good while yet. Because of his remove from and occasional antipathy to blackness, the Asian player can, in Van Gundy's unspoken racial economy, be cast as the racial minority.

Through Yao's protection by his white coach, the Asian athlete is not only represented metaphorically but subsumed into a collective, racially complicated, and victimized, proximate "whiteness." It is a whiteness produced out of his profession's complex racial logic. At the very least, Yao is situated outside of blackness, giving him access to a sui generis position in the NBA: the foreign player who is not white but is afforded the status of minority because he is not black. Because of the supposed evolution of the NBA into a post-racial black league, that space where blackness predominates so that it need not be (historically) named, African-American players do not have access to the discourse of "discrimination." The putative majority cannot be victimized by itself. Having borne the brunt of racism in the NBA's early years, African Americans are now protected from it. However, as the event of Ron Artest in November 2004 demonstrated, black bodies continue to be vulnerable in NBA arenas. After committing an intentional foul against the Detroit Pistons in their home arena in Auburn Hills,

the Indiana Pacers' Artest was involved in a scuffle
with the Pistons' center, Wallace. A fracas ensued and
Artest ended up supine on the scorer's table.
Momentarily at rest, Artest was attacked by Pistons
fans, the most vituperative of whom were overwhelm-
ingly white and drunk. That event, for which Artest
was fined $5 million and suspended for an unprece-
dented 73 games by the Commissioner, revealed that
despite their hegemony African-American players are
still located as "black"—which is to say recidivist—in
moments of crisis. Revealed in the comparison
between Yao and Artest is a signal difference, the
difference between how the Phantom operates for the
black and the Asian player: the black body is vulnerable to a physical, potentially career-ending white
violence, while the Asian body is subject to a symbolic
violence, the "bias" of the referee. The difference, that
is, between the end of a lucrative NBA career and a
bad call. However what is also drawn into question
here are the geographical and conceptual parameters
of "blackness:" does it incorporate into its majoritarian
position France's black guard Tony Parker or Haiti's
Eric Dalembert? Is Dikembe Mutombo of the
Democratic Republic of the Congo afforded the same
protection as the US Virgin Islands' Tim Duncan? Are
all blacknesses equal? Wasn't Ewing the African
American and Olajuwon the African in the 1980s and
'90s even though they both played on the 1992
American Dream Team at the Barcelona Olympics?

Following Jacques Rancière's thinking, Yao can
be understood as a subject outside the "dominant categories of identification and classification." He is also,

as we shall discuss later, a harbinger of the very process that will disarticulate what Rancière names the "established order" of economic things; in this instance, the disruption of the American "established order." However, where the event of the fouls may make Yao most efficacious as a distinctly racialized NBA player is in his capacity to highlight the historic "wrongs" and to draw into question the phantasmatic "equality" that is the post-racial NBA. In Rancière's terms, Yao inadvertently "created a common locus of dispute"—he makes race an issue in the NBA through his belonging that is not, and can never be, a full belonging. Not only is he a minority in the NBA, he is also outside of the dominant conception of what an NBA center should be.

It is Yao's antithetical relationship to the Phantom that explicates why Van Gundy's is, because of the conundrum of blackness, a racially and tactically complicated position. He cannot name the Phantom that is "racism" because to do so would be to imply that African-American players get, as it were, the calls; it would suggest they are not the victims of bad refereeing decisions in the same calculated way that Yao is. If Van Gundy charged NBA referees with racism, he would risk not only widespread public ire (of a very different kind), but also potentially alienate his own African-American players. How kindly would his star African-American guard, Tracy McGrady, take to being accused of inoculation from bad refereeing decisions because of his race? In order for Van Gundy to allege injustice he has to be aware of the parameters delineated by the Phantom. Van Gundy, especially because his whiteness makes his insinuations about racism suspect, is delimited by the presence of race. The most the coach can do is suggest that a particular mutation of racism is at work against Yao. Van Gundy has to rely on insinuation and nuance to do the work of political critique because he is himself disabled by his own racial location. Because he is not black, Yao does not have the same historic access to protection from racism; because the NBA has a racially complicated past that is not entirely passed, it has to insist upon itself as a post-racial, globalized enterprise that has transcended the inequities of its locality. The peculiar history of racism is everywhere and this is precisely why it cannot be spoken, even as it is strategically and rhetorically operative.

Americans in the NBA now routinely compete with and against other nationalities. However, Yao Ming represents a complication of this phenomenon. As the first foreign player who did not attend a US college to be taken at number one in the draft, he arrived in the NBA surrounded by an entirely different kind of hype than that which greeted the selection of an American high school graduate such as LeBron James. Moreover, the barely-ex Shanghai Shark was soon the target of an ethnically offensive remark by Shaquille O'Neal, the league's dominant player. Asked about playing against Yao on Fox Sports Network's *The Best Damn Sports Show Period*, Shaq shot back: "Tell Yao Ming: ching-chong-yang-wah-ah-soh."

Even before the Shaq brouhaha, Yao entered the NBA as an ethnicized and racialized subject. For his part, Yao seems fully aware of the dominance of

African Americans in the NBA, and of the role allotted to him in this racial drama. Yao did not respond to Shaq's ethnic taunting, dismissing it as nothing but typical NBA "trash talk." Asian-American cultural critics, on the other hand, were livid at O'Neal's disrespect to Yao—and by extension, to them. One of these commentators, Irwin Tang, invited Shaq to a "throwdown" in Chinatown. Commenting on the expectations symbolically imposed upon him by Asian Americans, Yao responded with a noticeable remove: "I sometimes think [Asian Americans] cheered for me when I came to the NBA not just because I was Chinese, but because they wanted me to be better than American players. It was as if they wanted me to punish US players for something other Americans had done to them. Maybe that was supposed to make them feel good, as though I was getting something back for them." Yao is, as we'll see, happy to bear the burden of over-representation for China. He will, however, have no truck with those whom he labels the "banana people:" "People in China call American-born Chinese ABCs and say that they are 'banana people'— yellow on the outside, white on the inside." As much as Yao rejects the "banana people," distancing himself from and refusing to own the Asian-American experience, the ways in which Van Gundy represents him as a model citizen of the NBA allows Yao to be momentarily interpolated into a certain kind of Asian-American "model minority" discourse.

In Van Gundy's estimation, Yao is "very easy to officiate, because no matter what you do, he's just going to walk to the other end... He's not going to make a stand. He's not going to get a technical foul. He's not going to kick a ball in the stands. And I applaud him for that. But he's also being taken advantage of for his kindness and his respect, and he's not being given the respect back." Van Gundy is representing Yao as the exemplary immigrant, the player who does not question authority, who plays by the rules even if the "law" is not always synonymous with justice; Yao's "discipline" is explicitly counterposed here to the "theatrical indiscipline" of other (African-American) players—those who "make a stand," "kick balls into the stands," or who refuse to "walk quietly to the other end" of the court. (Van Gundy's description of Yao recalls how Jackie Robinson would never vent his anger over racist taunts, in part because it was not his demeanor but also because Branch Rickey, the Dodgers' owner, warned Robinson against it. For his legendary restraint, Robinson was deemed by many to be, in the paternalistic jargon of the day, a "credit to his race.")

Again, Van Gundy raises the specter of race without actually using the term. Relying on the explicit comparison between those who respect the law and those who flout it, Van Gundy is able to mobilize the stereotype of the undisciplined African-American player—the Wallaces, the Iversons: black players known for the regularity with which they test, and occasionally transgress, the limits of the law. While Van Gundy will not directly address race, critics such as Larmer are prepared to identify the ghost: the threat of blackness. "To many observers, especially white fans watching the game from their suburban living rooms, Yao seemed the perfect antidote to the NBA's ills: a clean-cut, 1950s-style player who exuded humility rather than hubris." In the dying moment of the post-racial NBA dream, what is there for a white suburban fan to do but reach back nostalgically to the prelapsarian age? For the post-War innocence of the 1950s, when the league was a white league, symbolically if not literally, where authority was respected and the players, unlike their black contemporaries, knew their place? When humility—not hubris, and tattoos, cornrows, flashy jewelry, and incessant trash-talking— was the order of the day?

In the thwarted desire for the return to that historic moment, there is also the articulation of Yao as an "honorary white" player in the NBA. With the undisputed domination of African-American players in the NBA, white US players, to say nothing of white US stars, have become increasingly rare. Not quite an endangered species, but the sightings are few and far between. Into this racialized void has stepped, occasionally, the foreign player. Especially, we might add, the nondescript but effective white European recruit— the Pau Gasols (Spain), the Zydrunas Ilgauskases (Lithuania). By the end of the 1980s, Bird, Kevin McHale, Chris Mullin, and the ageless John Stockton were the nation's white stars. They were complemented by the likes of Smits and Schrempf.

Today, however, the only white "stars" are foreigners, such as the German Dirk Nowitzki and the South African-born, Canadian-raised, Steve Nash. These players have to bear the burden of white overrepresentation, a task for which they, to their credit,

appear to have little appetite. These foreigners reject
white America's ideological imposition, in part,
perhaps, because in a globalized league they each, like
Yao, already have a nationalist burden to bear.
Mexico's Eduardo Najera or Croatia's Toni Kukoc
might or might not want to publicly accept the burden
of national overrepresentation, but they are reminded
regularly, and often not by Americans, of their
"foreignness" in the NBA. It is not unusual, in the
various arenas where they play, to see Turkish flags
waved in honor of "Hedo" Turkoglu or a Serbian and
Montenegran section urging on Vlade Divac; when
Steve Nash of the Phoenix Suns returns to Canada to
play the Toronto Raptors, affiliations become really
twisted. Who do the Canadian fans root for? "Their"
(South African-born) star or "their" team (comprised
as it is entirely of Americans, from the coaches to the
players, except for Belize's Milt Palacio)? The immigrant communities in North America might each lay
claim to "their" star, much like Asian Americans have
symbolically named Yao as "theirs," but there is nothing simple about the politics of affiliation in the global
NBA, especially not for white European or South
American players who are simultaneously athletic
icons for the absent nation and, potentially, for the
white American fantasy of an athletic prowess that can
trump African-American hegemony in the league.
(Black players from Haiti or the Congo bear only, in
this regard, a single national burden. They can never
stand in for, or as, the "Great White Basketball
Hope.") All the while, of course, several of these
"international" players are massively enamored of the

culture—particularly the love for hip-hop music, the stylized dressing, and the tattoos—of black self-representation. Where does the foreign nation end and the immersion in a racialized Americanization begin? Can anyone play in the NBA and not become, to some extent, "American?" How are the "primary" allegiances to nation complicated by the condition of being a high-end gastarbeiter?

Devoid of tattoos, seemingly incapable of trash-talking, Yao is the very incarnation of humility. As a mode of athletic being, humility is grounded in the subsumption of the individual—the suppression of the colloquial ego—into the team project. The individual accomplishment, the logic of humility goes, matters only in so far as it serves the cause of the collective good. Recognized by journalists and fans alike as the consummate team player, Yao attributes his "self-diminishing" ethic to his basketball training in China: "Individual talent is everything in the NBA; that is different from China, where everything starts with teamwork." This narrative of self-sacrifice, of the subordination of the self, is what has made Yao such a white-fan favorite and corporate darling. Surrounded by his ego-driven African-American peers, Yao appears to give himself up willingly. Except, of course, that he is no different from them in his consciousness about his individual statistics (points scored, rebounds snagged, and so on), and attempts to secure a huge sneaker contract (Reebok) and other endorsements. Add to this his racial mutability and Yao is strategically positioned as the ultimate team player while simultaneously transcending it—by virtue of his height, his national origin, his dramatic entrance into the league, and, of course, his "humility."

Yao's racial mutability is especially important in the absence of a Great White Basketball Hope. If a white player can't be found, an Asian will just have to do. Yao may insist upon his Chinese-ness, but the limitations of his racialized agency are such that he can be made to represent desires and fill longstanding cultural and ideological vacancies that are far removed from his own. Yao's physiological Asian-ness does not preclude his ability to represent a symbolic whiteness. It is not only nature that abhors a vacuum but that white America cannot conceive of itself as an infinite athletic lack. Yao's is, in this politically charged way, not simply an "honorary whiteness" but a vitally necessary and strategic one too. Yao may conceive of himself as the inveterate team player, except that he could not have anticipated how many teams would lay claim to him as a member: the Sharks, the Rockets, the Chinese national side, Team White America, as well as China and Team Asia-America. To say nothing, of course, about the grand designs of Team Yao, the marketing machine that drives his branding.

In all his conformity to the team ethic, then, Yao evokes the condition of the model minority, the very discourse he so abhors. Yao instantiates, in the terms of Chinese cultural critic, Rey Chow, the "Protestant Ethnic." He is representative of the Asian immigrant who buys into the Puritan concept of hard work, self-sacrifice, and the honor in labor in order to secure a piece of the American Dream—which in Yao's case means a substantial share of NBA-generated

American capital. However, there are crucial ways in which the designation "model minority" might be conceptually inaccurate and inadequate to describe Yao's condition. Because he was already a star, even if it was only in the CBA, he does not really conform to the trajectory of the model minority. A true model minority would owe everything to the US, especially in the case of the political or economic refugee. For this model minority, its cultural, economic, and political achievements are a repudiation of the place of origin, that geo-political location that is not only oppressive but has also repressed the aesthetic potentiality of its erstwhile citizens. For the conventional narrative of the model minority, the immigrant-made-good, the US is the site of infinite possibility.

With Yao this trajectory does not apply. Because his propensity for labor and his skills derive from outside the US, the value added from his work ethic can be claimed by China. In this respect, Yao can more properly be conceived of as a variation on the classic Chinese "returnee:" that Chinese subject educated and trained in the US but ultimately in service to the Chinese nation. The returnee's role has been crucial to China's economic boom because of its skills, capital, access to technology and *guanxi* ("connections")—all vital to funding and sustaining China's massive economic growth; many enterprises in China owe their existence to returnee capital and expertise. In this configuration of the Chinese subject, Yao might best be understood as the "returnee-in-(advanced)-training," with the added bonus of the economic and cultural capital he is already responsible for making available to China. As part of the condition of his release from the Sharks, Yao agreed—what choice did he have, really?—to turn part of his NBA salary and his earnings from endorsements over to the CBA.

As the returnee rather than the model minority, Yao performs the kind of self-exclusion—repeatedly marking himself as Chinese, not as "Asian-American" or, worse, "American"—that is unimaginable to the model minority, for whom inclusion into America is the paramount psychological, cultural, and political concern. It is Yao's returnee status that motivates his steadfast refusal to become a "banana person." Even as he is ethnically slurred by Shaq, his physical and racial alter-ego, he will not take refuge in the bosom of the resident ethnics: those who presume to make a claim upon him culturally and politically, those who see him as constitutively of them without ever accounting for or understanding how immensely powerful Chinese sovereignty is, as a national identity, for Yao. The "returnee" keeps in place a sharp distinction between himself and the model minority.

However, Yao performs, as it were, the model minority discourse on the court even as he distances himself from it rhetorically. In his "soft," "non-physical" style of play, Yao raises the historical specter of the feminized male Asian body. His aversion to the combative nature of "playing inside," where "big men" such as Shaq, Duncan, and Wallace make their living, exacerbates his reputation as a player lacking toughness, physically and mentally. That "softness" (sometimes more perception than reality because Yao is,

sometimes, capable of asserting himself), even if it isn't
in a Shaq-like way), counterposes the feminized
"yellow" body to that of his hypermasculinized black
opponent. Even in Houston Rockets ranks, there is
the sense that Yao does not get calls, or, alternatively,
is often called against, because his "style" of play is not
combative enough. In the summer of 2005, for the
first time, Yao, instead of returning to China and playing with the national team (though he did do a little of
that), remained in Houston. The reason? To work out
against renowned NBA bruiser, the long since retired
but still up-for-a-scrap Moses Malone. The old stalwart's task was to toughen Yao up.

There is no euphemism for this: Yao is being
asked to play against type—to become more like a
black center. His Asian-ness, those outside skills, feminized him in the rough-and-tumble of the NBA inside,
and this made him vulnerable to bad calls by the
referee. Moreover, it is precisely his "model" behavior,
his refusal to contest calls or make his displeasure
public (which he perceived to be helping his team),
that makes him a liability for his teammates. Yao's soft
skills were not sufficient. He had to assume a physicality distinct and removed from his own. He had to de-
Asianize himself in order to maximize his value to the
team; he had to, as it were, become black in order to
really become a member of his team. Anything other
than that condemned him to a pseudo-effectiveness, a
difference that made him stand outside.

By employing Malone, Van Gundy was
acknowledging that in order for Yao to get the calls, to
"get respect," he has to physically and culturally

reconstruct himself; Chinese summer team workouts with CBA-caliber players simply would not do. Midway through the 2005-06 season, Yao's toughness was still a work in progress. Young centers, such as Eddy Curry of the New York Knicks, shoved him aside or drove on him relentlessly because Yao's is a body they do not fear. In fact, players such as Curry, to say nothing of veterans such as Shaq or Wallace, are often intent on initiating physical contact with Yao, confident that it is a battle the Chinese center cannot win.

The body of the athlete, which has a long history of standing as the body of the nation, is simultaneously reduced and magnified in the Yao event. In its micro-articulation (Asian-American), it is asked to refute the myth of the feminized ethnic by challenging—and redressing the historic wrongs endured—those "American" bodies that have dismissed the physicality of the Asian male. As a representative of the Chinese nation, Yao is expected to remain a national subject even as his basketball heritage seems difficult to unlearn and continues to disadvantage him in the NBA. According to CBA official Li Yuanwei, "I am not concerned that by playing in the NBA Yao Ming will develop a personality offensive to Chinese people." Which is, of course, by virtue of its denial, already an admission of concern. In his representation of the "Chinese people," Yao will not become an NBA—which is to say, "African-American"—player. He will not trash talk, he will not develop an "offensive personality," in more senses than one, and, to his detriment, he will not become more "physical."

Paradoxically, in remaining Chinese, Yao highlights the limitations of the CBA and the shortcomings of its players. He also, inadvertently, brings together the issues of physicality and aesthetics: is it Yao's body or his style that works against him?

Yao's "inadequate" body is expected to do triple duty when it's struggling to perform sufficiently for its smallest unit: the team, the Houston Rockets. For Yao, the national body—the Chinese national team—might be a site of respite from the demands of Asian-America, Asia, and, to a lesser extent, the Rockets. Little wonder then that Yao, in a purely physical sense, might take such pride in playing for the Chinese national team. There, at the very least, his body—his away from the basket style, his good passing and his "soft" hands, and his reputed lack of physical-ity—is adequate; there, his body is not called into question; there, the nation sees itself as splendid and not shoved around by the likes of Shaq, Wallace, and Jermaine O'Neal.

It's telling, however, how Yao used race to negotiate his location within the global through the ideology of the sovereign local. Even as he is familiar with the racialized history embedded in the vernacular speech of the African-American popular, for Yao race is an experience always vitiated by his Chinese-ness. "I know what 'nigger' means," he's said, "and I know that it's a bad word. When I first joined the Rockets, my teammates thought they heard Colin [Colin Pine, his translator] and me using it all the time. There is a word in Chinese that sounds a lot like it, but it doesn't mean the same thing. It really sounds like 'NAY-guh' and it means 'that' or 'that one' in Mandarin." Yao can translate race and racism into its local terms, but he will not transplant it from the globality of US discourse to the sovereignty of China. He will not allow for the mutation of "NAY-guh" into "nigger." Politics and economics, the site of sovereignty and the site of labor, have to be kept strictly apart. Never the twain shall meet. The Chinese nation militates against the universalization of US-style racism.

However, much as Yao—in ways that are very different from Jordan and Barkley—disavows race, he cannot be insulated from its workings. He is racialized in relation to his coach, by his coach's deliberate racial vocabulary (punctuated as it is by Van Gundy's telling silences), and his opponents (most publicly Shaq). Yao is, against his will, compelled into race and, in the process, serves as an unlikely progenitor of a new discourse of race. It is the sovereign national, participating in the flows of global capital, who internationalizes race while, inadvertently, deconstructing and exposing the myth of the NBA as a post-racial cultural practice. At the moment that he discriminates between "nigger" and "NAY-guh," at the moment that his coach protests "bias" not "racism," Yao is inducted into a discourse of race that makes race an issue that mediates, with an urgency utterly foreign to Kundera's landscapes, Houston and Shanghai. "NAY-guh" may not mean "nigger," but the globalized reverberations of the latter may overwhelm the linguistic difference articulated by the former.

Living with the Outcome:
Effects of the Age of Deng

> While marketization invariably swelled the wealth
> of a minority, democratization enfranchised whole
> populations only to put control back into the hands
> of elites.
>
> Harry Harootunian, *The Empire's New Clothes*

Because of how he is inserted into the discursive
history of the Phantom by his coach, Yao Ming is
dislocated into another set of racialized narratives.
The "phantom calls" reveal how the migrant Asian
subject of globalization is, in the moment of crisis or
the experience of direct address, precariously close to
the kind of non-belonging with which the raced

subject perpetually lives. Dislocation is rooted in the contingencies of partial affiliation to the cultural, political, and economic nexus in which the globalized subject labors. Race alone, in other words, cannot account politically for the Phantom. Race has to be thought of relationally and conjuncturally in its filiation to other categories of identity—gender, sexuality, class, ethnicity, and so on. Within the context of globalization, race is indissolubly linked to other categories of identity. It has to, furthermore, be understood as an articulation of the ideological complexities of the now.

Race is inextricably linked with the logics of space, temporality, US imperial desires and practices, the flows of global capital, and the Phantom of race/racism that is never past but is, in its historicity, always constitutive of the future-present. However, even in its most fluid concatenation, race demonstrates an arresting essentialism within these many "flows." Critics of essentialized identities have argued, with some validity, that the "flows" of globalization have done much to de-essentialize them. Because there is so much flux in the movement of the global subject, race, gender, sexual orientation and ethnicity are immobilized, stripped of the meanings that attached inveterately to them in earlier, more stable moments. Paradoxically, amidst all the movement that is innate to the basketball court, the ways in which the "fouls" called against Yao for his stasis is symptomatic of how, even within the relentless flow of global capital and diaspora, there is a moment of non-movement at which identity comes, for a brief but telling instant, to rest. There is a disruptive politics that attends to athletic bodies at rest—whether it is a Yao "pick" or an Artest laying vulnerable on the scorer's table in Detroit. Those essential categories of self articulate themselves emphatically in moments of stasis that are a precursor to the modality of crisis. In the moment of crisis, the self is addressed through the politics that attach to the Phantom, the essentialized self is publicly, viscerally available as the foundational category of political experience.

In the modality of crisis, the "black" or "ethnic" self is more publicly visible because the anxieties and fears it provokes makes a direct confrontation with that self inevitable. By going into the stands, Artest was instantaneously stripped of his status as NBA player and identified primarily as "black." Artest became, in that moment, the "undisciplined" product of the African-American inner city; he became the fulfillment of the symbolic "thug" that is only barely repressed on the court. There is, similarly, for Yao, the possibility that should a US-China crisis occur, the very Chinese-ness that he now so willingly embraces, a nationalist self-representation largely ignored by critics and fans alike, will be figured as a Communist or Chinese "threat" to America, in the process stripping his humility of its luster, and returning him fully to the status of Other. It is in the modality of crisis that the "essence" of the self becomes both a psycho-social space of refuge and the very articulation of a threat for others.

Even within the moment of crisis or intense self-recognition, however, the essential self cannot be thought of except in its multiple and complicated relations. Compelled by sovereign "bias" into a racialized conflict and an ethnicized and nationalized Chinese identity, the phantom calls disrupt the relations between race and globalization, between the figures of the exploited worker of global capital and the malevolent entrepreneur. Race is, of course, a key element—the only one of consequence, for some thinkers—in many critiques of the anti- or alternate globalization movement. However, linking Yao, multimillion-dollar basketball star, with race, dislocates the argument against globalization. It displaces the site of "exploitation" from the dimly lit factory in Southeast Asia to the over-resourced basketball arena in the US. (If, that is, "exploitation" can be conceived as the accumulation of US capital by the Chinese returnee.) The primary locales in the anti-global imaginary are the geographically peripheral but economically vital spaces: the sweatshop, the hovel-as-home-as-production-site, and the environmentally unsafe factory. These routinely minimal, frequently uninhabitable, spaces, function with the barest resources because capitalists look for low costs. The lower the overheads, the greater the profits: this is the girding logic of capital. Globalization articulates the asymmetrical relations between worker and capital, it makes manifest the material inequity that distinguishes the origin of capital from the site of its productive expansion and accumulation.

Within this scenario, Yao complicates the figure of the raced "worker" in the service of global capital. The discursive basis of the anti-globalization movement rests on the figure of the economically exploited, underpaid, underage, sexually harassed, predominantly female, and politically vulnerable worker. This figure is the postmodern, late-capitalist equivalent of the Industrial Age's Dickensian protagonist, that worker who as a matter of economic course puts in 18-hour days and is remunerated pennies. The racialized subject of capital is not, in the anti-globalization imaginary, located in the figure of the Shanghai worker-capitalist. This is less a contradictory than a complicated self-appellation that Yao, "returnee-in-training," claims for himself: "I still think of myself as a blue-collar worker. I sweat for my paycheck. If that makes me the best-known capitalist in China today, I don't have a problem with that." There is a complicated connection between Yao's self-perception and his actual relationship to capital. While he is willing to acknowledge himself as "capitalist," a self-designation that locates him squarely within the paradigm of Deng-era "socialism with Chinese characteristics" or, more accurately phrased, "capitalism with Chinese characteristics," Yao recognizes the insufficiency of that naming on its own. To admit his attachment to capital is one thing, an ideological naming permissible within a Chinese society that is increasingly competing with the US for domination in the global economy. What he cannot do, however, is have his capitalist predilections enunciated as his only Chinese identity.

Chinese society is, whatever its internal dissidents and external critics might suggest, still grappling, some thirty years later, with the transition from Mao Zedong's socialism and Cultural Revolution to

Deng Xioping's *xioakang* policies. Deng's "four modernizations," in agriculture, industry, education, and science and defense, introduced state-orchestrated capitalism into a China that had, since the revolution of 1949, been steadfastly socialist in its economic politics. As Rebecca Karl phrases it, "China is mired in a double timelessness: stuck in enmity toward the Mao period and yet with the Mao period appearing as an eternally repressed return." With the creation of "special economic zones" in coastal cities such as Shanghai and regions such as Guongdong, Chinese society has now for more than two decades been coming to terms with itself as a nation in ideological, political, and economic flux. Post-1978 China is laden with contradictions. It is increasingly a market for Western consumer goods, yet still rhetorically anti-American, deeply nationalist but more and more conscious of itself as a global force that through its proliferation blurs national identity.

The complexities and contradictions that mark the move from Mao to Deng, with all the attendant tensions and uncertainties, are thus given voice by Yao as he negotiates his identity between these two ideological poles: unrepentant capitalist and unreconstructed nationalist. In many ways, then, Yao is a prototypical representative of the Deng era. The basketball star, who makes at least $4.5 million a year in salary alone, is simultaneously marked by capitalist ambition and the residues of Mao's fierce socialist nationalism. However, when Eric Zhang, Yao's American-born Chinese agent, proclaims that "In the end, half the credit has to go to the macro environment made possible by the Chinese government's reform movement. Marketization, globalization, integration into the world—all of that made Yao Ming, NBA star, possible," he is only paying homage to Yao's Dengian heritage. Zhang's pronouncement could as easily have been Nike's Phil Knight or Microsoft's Bill Gates, so uncritically locked into the discourse is the agent, so publicly indebted to Deng's "reform" legacy are Yao and "Team Yao," as his advisors and handlers are known.

It is, however, precisely because Yao is more rooted in the lingering effects of Mao's revolution that he cannot simply locate himself unambiguously within the networks of neo-liberal global capitalism. He is not apologetic about his wealth, even though he is entirely unironic about representing himself as a "worker" who earns his living by the "sweat of his brow." The category of the "Chinese worker," to which Yao symbolically pledges allegiance, is nothing if not a Maoist construct—a Revolutionary identity that sits uncomfortably with the rhetoric and incomplete realities of a post-revolutionary, neo-liberal Chinese society. Yao's is an identity at odds with the neo-liberal project but entirely compatible with the logic of China as a national state that can accommodate itself to global capital without, it imagines, ceding sovereignty. It is this contradiction, full participation in the neo-liberal globalized economy while retaining sovereignty, which marks Yao as ideologically disjunctive within the context of the NBA. The NBA is a "national" association that no longer attaches great importance to any nation's sovereign boundaries.

In this regard Yao emerges as the heir to Mao, the "Great Helmsman," who will not acknowledge the Chairman except through muted denunciation: "There should be," Yao argues, "a balance between doing something for yourself and doing something for your country. The Cultural Revolution just took this idea too far. In some ways, it feels like history has played a joke on us Chinese." Basketball was one of Mao's great loves, in part because the Chairman believed that it was premised on values innately compatible with his Cultural Revolution: working hard and working for the team rather than the individual. Mao, like many a nationalist leader, also believed in bringing glory to the nation through sport. When Yao is nicknamed, in the Western media, as "Chairman Yao," it is meant to mark the public passing of the ideological torch from one Chinese political modality to another. In many respects, this celebration-of-neo-liberal-capitalist-triumph analysis is accurate. What it disregards, however, is how much of an accidental Maoist Yao is.

Like the "Great Helmsman," Yao believes in using his body in sport to bring honor to China, all the more so if those accomplishments are registered in the West that Mao abhorred and Yao admires from a proximate, nationalistic distance. Moreover, as the son of two basketball players, Yao is tall testament to Mao's gender-equity policy in sport. Mao believed that women and men should have equal access to sports opportunities, a policy that preceded the famed 1972 Title IX ruling in the US, which sought to level the field for women's collegiate sport. If "women held up half the sky," as Mao said, they should have the same access as their male counterparts to athletic competition. If Yao is, strictly in terms of talent, Da Fang and not Da Yao's son, then Mao could be configured, in terms of Yao's ideological lineage, as the figurative father. Mao is the father of the nation who made women's athletic participation and accomplishment possible, making the cultural and genetic birth of Yao, in turn, possible. It may be Mao, and not the diminutive Deng, hardly a basketball fan in the Mao mold, who engendered Yao.

Much as Yao was born in the Age of Deng, Mao's successor would have made an ironic father. At 4'11", Deng was so devoid of physical stature that his true height was treated as though it were a state secret. In photo-ops with visiting leaders, Deng decreed that he be shot from exactly the right angle in order to avoid embarrassing the Party leader. Phrased in Yao-ist terms, by age seven the future Shanghai Shark was already as tall as Deng. Little wonder, then, that even though it was Deng's reforms that facilitated Yao's entry to the West, it is Mao's ghost that haunts Yao's representation—especially in the West. The beneficiary of Deng's reform program, it is Mao's haunting presence—the leader his mother so loyally followed, for whom she was outcast from the Chinese sports establishment after his death, from whom "Yao," in English, is only a single consonant removed—that gives "Chairman Yao" such a strangely apt ideological ring. Even more than Wang, it may be Mao who is the biggest ghost in Yao's ideological machinery.

However, if Yao is in these compellingly contradictory ways the icon for the maturation of Deng's reform program, there should be no surprise that the multimillionaire basketball player should have been named, in 2005, one of 2,900 Chinese "model and advanced workers," an award ratified by China's State Council. Yao received this award in a ceremony at the Great Hall of the People, shortly before China's May Day celebrations. Not all Chinese workers were enamored of the decision to recognize such a citizen, and there was controversy—not difficult to understand, considering that the average Chinese worker makes just over $1,000 a year. The Maoist times, as Yao's newly minted status as model worker demonstrates, have long since changed even as the ghost of Mao continues to haunt Chinese politics, and the national basketball court in the person of a 7'6" Shanghai center. How else does the nation honor a "red capital-ist," that political category so deliciously, cruelly, laden with irony, but as a "worker"? Who could be a better "red capitalist" than Yao, the national worker who sweats profusely in his red uniforms? The son of the Red Guard in the Cultural Revolution has now mutated into an elite distinct from the kind that Mao inadvertently created. A globalized, transnational elite for whom the nation is still, à la Mao, central, even if it now lives at an economic remove.

We might then say, after Derrida, and even as we substitute our "Mao" for his "Marx," that:

> At a time when a new world disorder is attempting to install its neo-capitalism and neo-liberalism, no

> disavowal has managed to rid itself of all Marx's
> ghosts. Hegemony still organizes the repression
> and thus the confirmation of a haunting. Haunting
> belongs to the structure of every hegemony.

Neither "disavowal" nor silencing will rid "Chairman
Yao" of all Mao's ghosts. They haunt Yao even as neo-
capitalism and neo-liberal capitalism establish themselves as the new "disorder" in Chinese society. In
both a ghostly and a real sense, Mao has, like Marx,
found innumerable ways in which to survive himself.
This is how Yao's nationalist fervor complicates the
economic triumph of Deng's reforms. Following this
"reform" logic, it is appropriate that Yao should be
saluted as the exemplary gastarbeiter who faithfully
returns to the nation in his non-laboring summer.
"The reason why we nominated Yao," a Shanghai
work union official offered, "is that he shows the
modern image of the Chinese while being patriotic in
the international sports arena."

Yao takes every opportunity to make public his
patriotism, his commitment to China, an articulation
that distinguishes him from his American NBA
colleagues who are presumably not so enamored of
their nation-state: "I don't care how hard it is trying to
play for my country and in the NBA. If there's one
thing that bothers me, it's that not everybody thinks
about honor when it comes to the national team."
Yao's patriotism, however, is haunted by its own
Phantoms. In stark contrast to Yao's deep investment
in the sovereign nation there is the figure of the anti-
nationalist Chinese player, the athlete who does not

think about honor when it comes to playing for the team: Wang, Yao's old nemesis from the BaYi Rockets. Denied for two years the opportunity to join the Mavericks by the CBA, Wang struggled to adjust to the CBA. (It is hauntingly ironic that Wang should have been drafted by the Mavericks, the self-same team that would unleash—for, and via, Yao—the Phantom.) Instead of returning to China, as had been agreed by the Mavs and the CBA, Wang decided to stay in the US to work out at a summer camp for NBA players trying to improve their game. As in Yao's case, this was to toughen up because Wang had displayed the same liabilities as a center as Yao later would. Unlike Yao, Wang never "properly" informed the authorities in Beijing of his decision to miss the national team workouts, causing consternation. With his refusal to give his labor willingly and not to give of his capital to the nation, Wang condemned himself to be simply a capitalist, a capitalist without a red uniform.

Wang, the PLA lieutenant, had gone AWOL. The Chinese Army dispatched two of its officers to retrieve Wang, but to no avail as he easily escaped their attempts to escort him home. Even after he did meet with one of the PLA officers, he would not be persuaded to return—making Wang, in contrast to Yao, the "would-not-returnee." As Larmer summed it up, Wang was immediately "branded a traitor: kicked off the national team, vilified in the local press, expunged from the history books." Because he had, according to the authorities, caused China to "lose face" in full view of the world, he would be effaced from the nation's memory entirely. In the Yao-Wang conflict, Wang is not so much the tragic foil as the cultural prototype to be feared. Anti-heroes have their own magnetism, especially in a society where it seems that political turbulence is bubbling everywhere just below the surface.

Because of his de facto denunciation of Chinese sovereignty, and the nation's power to provide an individual's primary (political) identity, Wang now exists as a ghost within Chinese national team circles. He represents the irrecuperable figure, the player who has practically and symbolically renounced Chinese sovereignty, who has made public the (geo-political and cultural) limitations of China's hold over its citizens. Having denied the nation, he has been excised from it—he is now the "cannot-returnee." It was because of Wang's "defection" that it was so difficult for Yao to join the NBA. The CBA feared that it would lose another star to the West, symbolically if not literally, and so there was a great deal of last minute negotiating between the CBA and the Rockets. Yao did his part by signing the "loyalty pledge," a guarantee that he would not, as loyal citizen, cause the nation to "lose face" a second time in relation to the NBA. Yao wanted to follow in Wang's footsteps only in so far as he was determined to play in the NBA, but he would not bring shame upon the nation.

Unlike Yao, who abided strictly by his agreement with the CBA, Wang wanted no part of the strictures of Chinese nationalism or the Chinese national team after joining the NBA. Wang is the specter of defection that the CBA fears most: he is the

Phantom that haunts the past, the present, and the future of the CBA. In Wang, the CBA, with its heavy-handed officials, detects its own potential historical irrelevance. If more Chinese players follow the Wang rather than the Yao model of "graduating" to the NBA, loyalty to the self rather than the nation, the CBA will simply become—like all other national basketball associations—a feeder body. Wang represents the global trend, the Americanization of basketball, which the CBA is determinedly resisting. It is the Phantom of Wang that is not-so silently formative in Yao's insistent nationalism. There is, in the dialectical relationship between Wang's "dishonor" and Yao's "honor," a complex ideological interplay that emerges directly out of the ways in which globalization is, in individually symptomatic instances, prefiguring the demise of the CBA.

There are, however, other basketball and cultural factors at work outside of the "centers dialectic." For young Chinese basketball players, neither of these centers are players to be emulated, only in part because of their unusual height. There is a new breed of Chinese basketball player emerging, players such as Chen Jianghua, a point guard for whom the anti-hero has an especial appeal. Chen has modeled himself on the archetypal NBA "bad boy," AI, also known as Allen "The Answer" Iverson. He's the small guy who can play big, the little guard who has no fear of big men, the talented, feisty guard who relishes physical contact. Described by Larmer as, "Cool, irreverent, and the possessor of a style all his own," Chen has "more than a little of the young Iverson about him."

Just a few years younger than Yao, there is nothing dour about Chen. If the CBA thought Wang was a nightmare, it must consider Chen and his generation far more ominous. This is, unlike Wang's, a home-bred rebellion, complete with Philadelphia-style swagger and basketball braggadocio. Chen makes both Yao and Wang look old-school, Wayne Embry to his Allen Iverson.

The "rise of Chen" and the "irrelevance" of Yao are evident in the sale of NBA replica jerseys in China. In a market where Yao had dominated since his 2002 entry into the league, the old Shanghai Shark now finds himself trailing two of his NBA colleagues, neither of them centers. Moreover, Yao has lost "market share" to one of his own Rockets teammates: Tracy McGrady, star shooting guard, flamboyant, tattooed, and occasionally ill-tempered. It is likely that McGrady's status was enhanced by his promotional trip for Adidas to China in August 2005. Sandwiched between the two Houston Rockets is Chen's proto-type, "The Answer." That Iverson is an icon in China is not surprising (given how many NBA games are screened live annually in China), but the extent of his appeal is impressive since he is neither a national like Yao nor the beneficiary of a promotional tour like McGrady. Now approaching veteran status in the NBA, Iverson's time in America may well be passing, but the "AI" generation in China may just be getting started. It seems unlikely, however, that Chen will be signed by an NBA team. So far China is valued only for its big men, soft though they may be, and not its guards. In this case, ironically, for the CBA officials, the "big man" (Yao) is more easily controllable than the "small" guard.

Chen and his generation are the Phantoms that Yao, full-blooded offspring of Deng and Mao, is being asked to keep at bay by the CBA. In a strangely understandable way, Yao is now under less pressure to repudiate Wang than he is to counteract Chen and foreclose the new generation's aesthetic and athletic rebellion. After all, what good is the model basketball worker if he cannot stay the "Second Cultural Revolution" at home? Unknowingly, between them, the center Wang and the guard Chen have put tremendous pressure on Yao's cultural identity, on his ideologically burdened role in Chinese socio-political life, at home and abroad.

Identity politics creates an uncanny nexus of class, race, patriotic citizenship, and ethnicity. Race, citizenship, and class articulate each other across categories and the vast expanse of geographical and ideological distance—if, that is, one does not designate China's "socialism" as entirely subsumed by the logic of neo-liberalism. Ever alert to the contradictions of his award, and cogniscent of its determinedly working-class (in an old fashioned Marxist sense) history, Yao tries simultaneously to respect that history and to refigure it for the realities of post-Deng Chinese neo-liberalism: "I used to think that model worker was a title for those ordinary laborers working hard... but now, apart from them, special 'migrant workers' like me can also be awarded." In a less than deft ideological maneuver, Yao tries both to praise the "ordinary workers" and to point to the new economic realities that he, from his lofty perch, instantiates. New categories are required for new moments, for "migrant workers" who are nothing if not "special." Those who are not special have reserved for them a very different designation: the traitorous (haunting) Phantom. Which takes care of the past (Wang), but what of the future (Chen)?

How does China and the CBA deal with the displacement of Jordan by "The Answer" as the US icon of choice? When post-racialism is replaced by an unapologetic blackness? When the unmarked post-race body is rejected in favor of the extensively tattooed one? What happens when it's passé to be like Mike and Yao (and so soon, too), and a whole generation wants to be like AI? That's the moment of the now, the moment that it is culturally, aesthetically, athletically, and ideologically time to recognize: there's a whole new ball game in this big Asian town, revealing a complex racial logic. White American suburbia and the CBA's worst case scenario, AI, representative par excellence of a particularly black way of NBA being, represents the new generation of Chinese basketball's greatest desire. One wonders if the CBA knew what it was opening the door to when it let Wang, Bateer, and Yao go to the NBA. Did anyone, Stern perhaps, not tell them that the post-racial NBA was about to go the way of George Mikan's canvas sneakers?

Anti-Americanism, Sui Generis

If China was a late-comer to the process of neo-liberal globalization, it has made up ground fast. So fast, in fact, that it is now the most serious threat to US global economic domination. It is crucial, for this reason, that the event of the Phantom turns on the figure of a Chinese basketball player. In the American neo-liberal, imperial imaginary, China is both what is most intensely desired and what is most greatly feared. With its unrivaled population, its rapidly growing middle class, and its expanding markets, China represents the last—and most lucrative—frontier for global capital. However, as critics from David Harvey to Giovanni Arrighi to Rebecca Karl warn, it is also the hegemon to come, the global power that will displace America from its dominant position and reorder the location, functioning, and control of global capital. For this reason, writing from the West, it does appear that if the dream of the American empire for the New Century is going to flounder, it is in all likelihood going to do so on the "rock" that is the Great Wall. The economic Great Wall, that is, not the now-dissolved basketball one.

> As frequent targets of direct or indirect American and imperialist violence over the past century, [the Chinese] have rarely fallen under the illusion of America's original state of grace, or its unfailing "good intentions."

Karl writes this within the context of a discussion about anti-Americanism, an old political trope that is not unexpected, given the grandiose ambitions of the US empire, finding urgent new articulations. If China has long been, like many nations around the world, anti-American, it is also distinct in the new century. China is different, in part, because of its burgeoning economic prowess, and because of an antagonistic history with the US. Equally important, as Harvey argues,

> China is not dominated by the United States in the same way as Japan and has the capacity and, at times it seems, the willingness to take on a territorial leadership role within the region as a whole.

This is what makes China's anti-Americanism sui generis: it speaks from a position of increasing economic strength and political authority. Unlike historically anti-Americans, such as the French, who operate from a position of increasing national decline in relation to America, the Chinese are positioning themselves with ever-growing confidence as the heirs apparent to the neo-liberal empire.

While the French bemoan their loss of influence in international politics, the erosion of their culture by Hollywood and McDonalds, and the recognition that their language has for decades been losing ground to English, the Chinese watch their markets grow, their direct foreign investment rise dramatically, and their political clout increase as they situate themselves as the only nation powerful and determined enough to oppose imperial wars in the Middle East—wars, of course, in which China has its own vested interests as it seeks to maintain relations with nations that can supply oil to meet its ever-growing demand for energy.

As a metonym of China's specific relationship to globalization, Yao represents a very specific articulation of that phenomenon on the NBA court. Yao represents an entirely new figure in the history of capital. Hannah Arendt famously argued that the refugee is the paradigmatic figure of modernity—the "citizen of the nowhere" who demonstrates the incapacity of national sovereignty to absorb into its territoriality any subject other than its citizens. It is the refugee, the "vanguard of their peoples," who presages the coming of the others who are not yet here but soon will be—that is what the arrival of the refugee, and the colonial and postcolonial immigrant, intimates. That is the threat it contains in its coming. In our age—marked by crisis, wars, natural disasters, persecution, ethnic cleansing—the refugee is increasingly commonplace, representing, as it were, the era of the post-citizen in which we live our history.

The refugee is, decidedly, not the category to which the "returnee-in-training" Yao, or any other skilled NBA gastarbeiter, belongs. Yao is the incarnation of a different, historically unprecedented figure: the advance representative of Chinese globality. He is the anticipated figure that is already toweringly present. Yao is the most culturally visible emissary of Chinese globality that announces, in all its fissured, contradictory, complexity, the coming of the "consolidated" (Chinese) nation to international dominance. He may be figured, in the US and Western media in general, as the "giant with the friendly face," but he is a giant nonetheless.

It is Yao's "coming" that has rendered obsolete the old-style, Cold-War Pentagon concerns about "who lost China." Those anxieties have mutated into, for Nike, McDonalds, IBM, Microsoft, GM and the like, a much more ambitious project: who will win China? But that supposition is foolhardy in the extreme, and its proponents, instinctively if not articulately, know that. The real Chinese Phantom that Yao's subjectivity as nationalist-globalist articulates, is more disturbing to US imperial ambitions. Yao represents a China that is now, for the first time since the Cold War began, only secondarily an ideological foe. This lofty son of Deng and Mao has made redundant the "who lost China?" mode. China is now primarily feared because it is the US's most powerful economic competitor. Economics have triumphed over ideology, if we ignore for a moment how constitutively ideological all economic practice is.

Symbolically, this is why Yao is different from NBA players such as Argentina's Ganobli or France's Parker. As NBA competitors they can be spatially contained to the NBA court; Argentina and France can be, for all ideological intents and purposes, disregarded, unless you're in the business of winning an NBA championship, that is. China (if not Yao), it is feared, cannot be similarly curtailed. Who would have imagined that James Naismith's cultural export of a hundred years ago, then the product of an American empire still in its infancy, would return to these shores as a Phantom? A cultural spectacle symbolizing powerful economic clout? As the incarnation of the strangely familiar? The project of Deng's heirs in the boardrooms of China's state corporations is now the inverse of those debated in the halls of the Pentagon after Mao's revolution. Who will win America?

What happens to China if it "wins" America? This inquiry is especially loaded because of what has already taken place in China as a result of its "transition." As Harvey points out, China has already confronted the US on several international fronts, disagreeing at the UN, refusing to kowtow like Britain and the rest of the EU, and it has certainly never shown any signs of being beholden like Japan or South Korea. However, if Wang and Chen are, in their very distinct ways, anything to go by, the limits of Chinese sovereignty may not be the now booming economy, its military might, or the Tiananmen-like political repression. It may be, then, paradoxically, not the economy, but, to ironize George H.W. Bush, that well known Sinologist, *the culture, stupid*.

"The Dark Side of the Moon"

> ...a global labor movement has yet to take shape,
> while the evidence of cooperation and collusion
> between transnational capital and the nation-state
> is everywhere.
>
> Theodore Huters, *China's New Order*

Metaphorically, the "foul" calls against Yao released
more than one Phantom into public articulation. It
was not simply the local, unfriendly ghost of race,
returning to haunt one of America's foremost cultural
practices, basketball, or the anti-sovereignty ghost that
was loosed in China. His silent, impeccable on-court
demeanor notwithstanding, Yao represents the spectral
presence of Chinese capital within America. He is,

precisely because of his complicated ideological heritage, the most profound threat to American empire. Yao believes in national sovereignty, unlike the highly individuated and individualized American athletes with and against whom he competes. It is for him not only an honor to represent his country but a burden of over-representation that he willingly assumes and does so to counteract the Phantom of Wang and to postpone, as long as he can, the rise of the Chen generation, a Phantom that, like many Phantoms, can never be properly named even when it has an all too publicly recognizable proper name: "Maybe this is only in my head, but sometimes I feel as if I'm carrying those millions of Chinese with me, that my failure will be their failure." China's propensity for globalization, for participating in the neo-liberal world economy is, for Yao, grounded firmly in the sovereignty of the nation.

If US globalization has increasingly deconstructed and diluted its sovereignty, Yao insists upon a Chinese global advancement premised on fealty to the nation. China's economic transition succeeded, in the view of Washington Consensus critics like Joseph Stiglitz, precisely because of its insistence upon its sovereignty, which he names "gradualism" in *Globalization and its Discontents*. Economic transformation worked in China because it refused to follow the neo-imperialist dictates of the IMF. Like Poland, another IMF refusenik, China was able to make a successful transition to a market economy because it "protected" its sovereignty better than, say, South Korea. As a result, it "thrived"—as the Polish economy can also be said to be doing—by following its own economic policies because it, and not the Washington Consensus bureaucrats, knew what was best for its people, what hardships could be endured, which not. China and Poland are consequently not as beholden to the IMF, as many other nations in the developing world are, in perpetuity.

However, as Chinese workers are already finding, with the loss of jobs, the degradation of the environment, and the return of an elite economic class, there is a backbreaking price to pay for leading, as critics have charged, this "race to the bottom." There is a tremendous cost to the Chinese workers for what global corporations call the "China price." According to Ted Fishman, the "*China price* has since become interchangeable with lowest possible price. China has become a cut-rate El Dorado, where the lowest prices are gold." The post-Mao era has witnessed, writes Chinese leftist Wang Hui in *China's New Order*,

> corruption, the smuggling, the unfair distribution, the influence of interest groups on public policy, the overdevelopment (as with real estate in Shanghai, Huan and other places), and the resulting financial crises, problems with the social welfare system, environmental concerns and the like.

There are many reasons, as Wang Hui's litany enumerates, for caution about China's "new order." Now in the midst of the largest migration in human history, many of the migrants from the devastated rural areas who have been flocking to the cities for more than a decade, are—following Anita Chan—the "main victims of the most serious labor-rights violations."

These migrants, 300 million at latest count in 2005, up from just 80 million in 1999, instantiate what Andrew Ross names the "low wages, high profile" phenomenon. Except, of course, that for this, the most vulnerable economic constituency in China, "low wages" would be a vast improvement over what is frequently their fiscal reality: no wages, unpaid labor to "workers" slaving away in prison-like compounds. Many of these compounds are located on the outskirts of cities at the hub of the Special Economic Zones that drive the new Chinese econ-omy. Because of their centrality to the nation's econ-omy, the injustices done to Chinese workers has given them the highest global profile of any nation's exploited—the "low wage" folks are the dastardly face of China's "new order," an order that presides over one of the most unequal societies in the world. In China inequity means more because it is the most populous nation on the planet. Here economic discrepancy may have serious global consequences. These migrants, many of them undocumented, many of them not allowed access, unlike the legal residents of the cities, to education for their children, or healthcare for themselves, and devoid of any real access to protection under the law, represent a real threat to the Chinese authorities because they consti-tute what has come to be called a "roving nation."

They are marching, as it were, from the impoverished rural backwaters to the cities in search of employment, in search of a better life not only for themselves but for their families who rely on remittances not yet earned. The 300 million strong "roving nation," with its apparently incessant movement from Chinese city to Chinese city, raises its own historic specter. Beginning, like that other, memorably arduous trek, from the rural hinterland to the nationalist cities, one is almost compelled, by ghostly force, to ask: is this, with its own historical particularities, the second incarnation of the Long March? How will they effect not only Arrighi's and Harvey's predictions but the CP's capacity to "manage" the nation's economy and its political future?

These factors introduce a note of caution into the conversation about China's role in globalization's future. And a certain unpredictability, too. After all, while China has the biggest markets, boasts the largest growth, attracts the greatest amount of foreign investment, has the largest savings, and the biggest, most "docile, disciplined" workforce in the world, its economy is, more than most, tied to global financial markets. China's economy may be "exceptional" in many ways, but it is worth remembering that Japan and the Asian Tigers were also once thought exemplary because of many of these self-same qualities. As the 1997 Asian crisis demonstrated, China is not exempt from the booms, busts, inflation, and stagnation of the global economy, even if it did recover more quickly than any of its Asian neighbors. It is China's very integration into, and therefore vulnerability to, the world economy that throws into relief the older historical model of the US declining and China rising. Like all other economies, China's is "dependent" on the US market—more so, arguably, because of all those US Treasury bonds that China owns. What happens to the Chinese economy if the US dollar plunges? Is it possible that a future market will—what with the simultaneous emergence of massive Chinese and Indian middle classes—mitigate against domination by a single power?

Moreover, once it became a key player in the global economy, it made itself ideologically vulnerable. China invited a confrontation with the limits of its (political) sovereignty. Metaphorically, there may have been something prescient in Deng's oft-quoted saying. Doing his rhetorical best to reconcile Chinese socialism with the capitalism his reforms initiated, Deng remarked: "It doesn't matter if the cat is black or white as long as it catches mice." The color of the feline might not matter, but letting the ideological cat out of the bag certainly does. Just take a look, if you will, at what happened when a certain Army lieutenant was, in Dengian terms, let out of the bag. That certainly set the cat among the CBA and PLA pigeons, didn't it? So much so that Yao had to swear he too wouldn't run away if he was allowed to "catch" the "mouse" that is the US dollar.

Even from this single example it is evident that China's role in the global economy moves at a different speed than the political changes affected by such fiscal developments. The US declining/China rising narrative functions in a different way on a cultural and ideological level—where it is animated more on an affective level by fear and anxiety and less on an economic level. As much as these two levels permeate and inform each other, it is crucial to be mindful of their discreteness because such a "conceptual separation" allows for the opening up into a new set of political and paradigmatic possibilities. In this way, Yao's affective attachment to the nation can be understood as the complex source of, simultaneously, economic certitude and ideological uncertainty.

A first generation Dengite, Yao may represent the last generation that is so steadfast in its patriotism, so deeply attached to Chinese sovereignty. As prefigured in Wang, the time of Yao's generation may already be passing. It may be an identity, a form of Chineseness that is no longer tenable for the next generation: those displaced workers, those rural Chinese who have not and cannot participate in the globalized economy that has rewarded Yao both within and outside China.

The road from Shanghai to Houston, from the Sharks to the Rockets, may have been facilitated by Deng's reforms. It may, however, have had a more circuitous, American beginning. Springfield, Massachusetts is, in geo-political and cultural terms, the proper origin of Yao's trajectory. In that early articulation of American empire, there was, then, basketball—what can now be read as the harbinger of the new order of globalization. There was no way in which James Naismith anticipated a "big man" as dominant as Mikan. Naismith certainly did not forsee African-American stars such as Russell or Wilt or Dr. J. He could not have had the prescience to imagine a Michael Jordan.

Nor could Naismith have envisaged a moment in which there would be an international racial event on a US basketball court that involved a white coach defending his Asian player against the hegemony of African Americans. In his imaginary, the most Naismith could have conceptualized was an African-American team such as the Globetrotters or the Rens playing an all-white Celtics or Knicks side. It would not have been possible for him to believe that the sport he created would be exported to Asia and then return, more than a century later, as the Phantom that would provoke such animated political discourse about race.

It is race that at once connects and distinguishes the new road from Shanghai to Houston from the previous one from Springfield to Shanghai. Whereas the basketball journey to Shanghai was undertaken against a backdrop where the exclusion of the black body from the American cultural public sphere was still possible, the road leading from Shanghai denies such a repression—even in its post-racist, post-racial articulation. With the event of Yao, the full light of the dark side of the moon has been shone on race. It is in this way that a Chinese player illuminates the discourse about racism, not only in the US but also in China. Houston and Shanghai each have their own Phantoms, Phantoms that are rudely unleashed in a way that reveals—to the surprise of the NBA or CBA basketball commentator—how much of that Phantom goes by the name of racism. It is, finally, the double historical repression of race that links Shanghai to Houston, that reveals the road to the NBA to run not so much from Springfield to Houston but through a more singular, globalized local phenomenon: the phantasmatic event of the black body. The black bodies to which the YMCA did not minister, did not attempt to proselytize, the black athletic bodies that Clifton stood in for, and the black imaginary named "Iverson" that Chen, much more so than Yao, understands in its full antagonistic complexity.

An act of injustice done to a Chinese player in the US can, we might suggest, assume an ideological import that goes way beyond the game. The NBA may be able to punish Jeff Van Gundy, but it is doubtful whether American capital can discipline or contain the expansion of Chinese economic dominance for very much longer. Who knows what Maoist propensities lurk in the age of Hu Jintao? Who knows how the "March of the Roving Nation" will end? Or, where it will end. Who can tell whether or not the "Roving Nation" will come into direct conflict with the CP Nation? What would the consequences of such a challenge to the nation be?

Phantoms, we should have learned, are uncanny in their historical capacities. When the phantasmatic is called into public articulation, it can speak in instructive ways. As Hamlet found out, to his considerable cost: ghosts are best listened to. To ignore them is fatal. ■

Acknowledgements

My thanks to Matthew Engelke who commissioned this pamphlet. He is as good and trusting a sight-unseen, long distance editor as anyone can ask for. I could not have written this without his keen editorial hand. I owe Andrew Ross one more debt: for reading the draft with his customary insight and asking, as he always seems to do, just the right questions. Tess Chakkalakal offered a sharp critique, opening new directions for the project. Thanks also to Steve Walk and David Andrews of the North American Society for the Sociology of Sport who first invited me to present the earlier version of this work as their keynote address in 2005. To my research assistant, Jennifer Rhee, for her thorough and imaginative probings. To the Toronto B-boys: Ian Balfour and Eric Cazdyn: Raptors lovers, hip-cool theorists.

To the kids: Andrea Farred: for her unfailingly "bad attitude." To Alex Juffer: Allen Iverson fan, State College "bad boy."

My greatest debt is to Jane Juffer for reading innumerable drafts of the pamphlet with patience and love. In addition to her wonderful shooting touch, she brought to *Phantom Calls* her generous intelligence and her deep passion for the game.

Also available from Prickly Paradigm Press:

continued